IN TIME
and
WITH LOVE

Other books by Marilyn Segal, Ph.D.

Your Child At Play: Birth to One Year
Your Child at Play: One to Two Years
Your Child at Play: Two to Three Years
Your Child at Play: Three to Five Years
(with Don Adcock, Ph.D.)

Making Friends
Play Together Grow Together
All About Child Care
Just Pretending

IN TIME
and
WITH LOVE

Caring for
the Special Needs Baby

Marilyn Segal, Ph.D.

Newmarket Press
New York

88 89 90 M-V 10 9 8 7 6 5 4 3 2 1 HC

88 89 90 M-V 10 9 8 7 6 5 4 3 2 1 PB

Library of Congress Cataloging-in-Publication Data

Segal, Marilyn M.
In time and with love.

Bibliography: p.
Discography: p.
Includes index.
1. Handicapped children—Care—United States—
Handbooks, manuals, etc. 2. Problem children—Care—
United States—Handbooks, manuals, etc. 3. Developmentally
disabled children—Care—United States—Handbooks,
manuals, etc. 4. Child rearing—United States—Handbooks,
manuals, etc. I. Title.
HQ773.6.S44 1988   649'.151   87-34711
ISBN 0-937858-95-1
ISBN 0-937858-96-X (pbk.)

Quantity Purchases

Companies, professional groups, clubs and other organizations
may qualify for special terms when ordering quanitities of this title.
For information contact: Special Sales Dept., Newmarket Press,
18 East 48th Street, New York, New York 10017, or call
(212) 832-3575.

Manufactured in the United States of America

First Edition

To my daughter,
Debbie Segal,
who has helped me
understand the importance of time and of love.

Contents

Acknowledgments

I would like to thank the following people who made substantial contributions to *In Time and With Love*.

Lorraine Greenhill has served as parent coordinator and discussion leader for Ring-A-Round, an early intervention program for families with young handicapped children sponsored by the Family Center at Nova University. Lorraine conducted the individual interviews of family members and led the group discussions that provided source material for *In Time and With Love*. Through her empathy and skill she has helped parents share their feelings and has elicited many of the insights and quotations included in the book.

Roni Leiderman, Ph.D., associate director of the Family Center and director of the Infant Ring-A-Round Program, has been responsible for developing and testing many of the parent/child games described in the activity section. She cheerfully and tirelessly arranged for all the photographs and gathered material for the appendixes.

Barbara Lloyd, coordinator of the Ring-A-Round Program, has been involved in the development of this book from the beginning. She interviewed parents, reviewed the research, and contributed portions of the text in several chapters. Her ability to tune into parents and understand their concerns make her contributions especially valuable.

Wendy Masi, Ph.D., associate director of the Family Center and coordinator of the Early Learning Center, served as my harshest and most perceptive critic, reading and enhancing the book.

Jack Mills, Sc.D., read and reread the manuscript, rewording and inserting ideas. He shared his expertise on language development and his gentle and sensitive understanding of parents under stress.

Edward Saltzman, M.D., Robert Schultz, M.D., and Richard Auerbach, M.D., generously shared their time, experience, and expertise. They described with insight and sensitivity the dynamics of parent/professional relationships.

The parents, grandparents, and babies in the Ring-A-Round Program and the Early Learning Center have been the primary resource for *In Time and With Love*. They shared their good and bad experiences and talked honestly about their pain, their joy, their frustrations, and their dreams.

IN TIME
and
WITH LOVE

Introduction

I have been on both sides of the fence. First, as the parent of a handicapped child, I have struggled with grief, pain, hope, and despair. I have desperately searched for a doctor who could tell me my baby would be fine. Second, as a developmental psychologist, I have watched parents walk out of my office disappointed and angered by my inability to put their fears to rest. Both as a parent and as a professional I have accepted the fact that there are questions that cannot be answered and problems that cannot be solved. At the same time I have recognized the need for an authoritative handbook that would help parents mobilize their resources and build on the strengths of their baby even when there are no firm answers.

In Time and With Love is written for parents whose baby is handicapped, developmentally delayed, or constitutionally difficult. It is very much a collaborative effort. It draws on my knowledge and experience as a mother and a developmental psychologist. It draws on the expertise of the staff of the Family Center at Nova University who work with parents and babies on a daily basis. Most importantly it draws on the experience and expertise of 24 families with special needs babies who took part in an interview study.

The parents who participated in the interview study were enrolled in the Ring-A-Round Program, an early intervention and support group sponsored by the Nova University Family Center. The study included individual interviews of Ring-A-Round family members as well as a series of group discussions. The interviews were designed to explore the impact of a handicapped or difficult baby on different members of the family. The group discussions tapped parental perspectives as to what the book should include and how it should be presented.

In the first group discussion we asked parents to describe the kind of parenting book that they thought we should write. Did they envisage a book that dealt primarily with their own experience parenting a handicapped infant, or did they feel the book should be more of a how-to guide for parenting? We were surprised by how much agreement there was. The book, they said, should include both perspectives. It should help parents understand and deal with their own feelings and should also provide accurate information and practical suggestions. Above all, the book should present an honest picture of what it is like to live with a problem baby: "Don't make it all rosy," they advised, "but don't make it heavy and dismal either."

One of the first questions we asked parents was about the audience for the book. Should this book be strictly for parents whose babies are diagnosed as handicapped, or should we write a book for a wider audience of parents with difficult babies? Based on their own experience, parents made a strong point of avoiding diagnostic categories: "Don't get hung up on labels. A sleeping problem is a sleeping problem whether the baby is premature or has Down syndrome. If you provide practical information on taking care of babies, parents can decide for themselves whether the book is for them."

In accordance with the advice of parents, *In Time and With Love* is written for parents who have concerns about their baby's early development. These concerns may relate to a diagnosed problem or a difficult beginning, or they may relate to problem behaviors or delays in development that have no explanation. Unfortunately, or perhaps fortunately, there is no good label for such babies. Whether we characterize babies as handicapped, disabled, developmentally different, at-risk, having special needs, limited, or problematic, the label is nondescriptive and in many cases inappropriate. Our imperfect solution has been to use a variety of terms and hope that readers will not be troubled by the labels.

Most of the subsequent discussions were devoted to the contents and organization of the book. The group talked about dividing the book into clearly designated sections so that parents could use the book as a reference without reading it from cover to cover.

Part I of *In Time and With Love* is devoted to exploring emotions. In the first chapter parents share their feelings about having a disabled infant. They talk about the worst and the best times and describe how a growing love affair with their baby softens negative feelings. In the next four chapters we look at the impact that a child with a disability has on family and social relationships. In each chapter we describe adaptive ways of coping with stress and emphasize the importance of seeking and accepting support.

Part II focuses on the daily interactions between parents and infants. Chapter 6, "Reading Your Baby's Cues," describes ways of recognizing and responding to your baby's unique temperamental and behavioral characteristics. Chapter 7 examines the routines of daily living with a special needs baby: sleeping, eating, diaper changing, dressing, and bathing. Chapter 8 is devoted to social skill development and the management of problem behaviors.

Part III explores games and activities that help parents and infants learn from each other. Chapter 9 focuses on social and emotional development and suggests a variety of ways parents can communicate with their children and support their emerging self-awareness. Chapter 10 describes the development of motor skills and suggests playful ways to help babies develop balance, strength, and coordination. Chapter 11 covers language development and offers games and activities for helping babies tune into the sounds, meaning, and functions of language. Chapter 12 presents activities that promote the development of problem-solving skills.

Part IV, Decision Making, examines the many decisions that parents of handicapped children must make in the first two or three years of their baby's life. Chapter 13 is devoted to selecting and interacting with physicians, therapists, and other professionals. Chapter 14 addresses the tough questions that parents often face: "Should I have another baby?" "Should I send my baby to school?" "Should I search for a different doctor or a more effective program?" "How should I plan for the future?"

Part V is a resource guide for parents. It contains a listing of parent organizations, parent publications, professional organizations, books to read to children, and recommended toys and equipment. It also includes brief explanations of the medical procedures and developmental tests commonly used with at-risk or handicapped babies.

Although *In Time and With Love* deals with babies who have a variety of developmental difficulties, we make no attempt to describe specific syndromes or diagnostic categories. This omission is deliberate. In working with babies who fall into diagnostic categories, we have been struck much more by their individual differences than by how they are alike. Our hope is that the approach we have chosen for *In Time and With Love* will help parents tune into their baby's unique qualities and gain an intimate knowledge of their baby's needs and strengths.

PART I

A TIME FOR ADJUSTMENT

"Make me one promise. If you're going to write a book for parents of handicapped babies, say it like it is—with the bad stuff as well as the good stuff. And don't give me that line about how I was chosen by the angels to be the mother of God's special child."

"I don't need a book to tell me how bad I feel. If I'm going to read a book I want it to give me a lift—I want to read about hope, about looking on the bright side, about the cloud with a silver lining."

In Part I of *In Time and With Love* the focus is on coping skills. The first chapter, "Finding Out," explores how parents respond when they learn that their baby has a physical problem. Chapter 2, "Marriage Under Stress," deals with both positive and negative changes in partner relationships. Chapter 3 discusses the role of grandparents and in-laws; we see how a child with a problem can tear a family apart, or bring it closer together. Chapter 4, "Siblings," examines how older and younger children cope with jealousy and befriend the disabled child. Chapter 5 considers ways families reach out to gain support by broadening their circle of friends.

The purpose of this section is to help parents confront their feelings honestly and to recognize that anger, ambivalence, and self-pity are common and natural emotions that every parent shares. We also want parents to recognize that, despite the negative feelings, parenting a handicapped child provides many tender and wonderful moments. The experience can mobilize untapped strength, providing insight into our own lives and those of other parents.

CHAPTER

1

Finding Out

"I felt angry—like God was getting back at me for something. But I couldn't think of anything I had done that was so horrible. I kept thinking, 'Why me?'"

The turmoil that parents experience when they first find out that their baby has a problem has been described in many ways. Some professionals talk about a period of bereavement in which parents face the loss of the perfect baby dreamed about during pregnancy. Others distinguish a predictable sequence of emotions. First there is denial: "The doctors must be mistaken." Next there is anger: "Why did God let me down?" Then comes depression: "For the rest of our lives we'll be burdened." Finally there is reconciliation: "He's our baby, and we love him."

In this chapter we look at the pain and grief of finding out; we also look at healing. We listen to parents who live with a special needs baby describe their conflicting feelings, which are often disguised. As parents let down their guard and talk about dark thoughts, others may recognize that their own hidden feelings are neither unique nor shameful. Love and hate, pain and pleasure, joy and sorrow are all commingled. The same baby who gives the deepest pain can bring the most intense pleasure.

As a way of exploring the emotional experience of parents with handicapped infants, the author conducted a series of individual and group interviews. The interviewees included mothers, fathers, grandparents, and siblings. As parents talked about the emotional turmoil they had been through, they described painful and disturbing experiences over and over again. Despite this common theme, each family's experience was personal and unique.

Grief and Loss

To explain their initial feelings about their child's problems, many parents went back to their pregnancy and talked about their dreams and expectations: "I felt so close to my baby during pregnancy, listening to his heart beat, feeling his kicks. But the damaged baby I gave birth to was not the baby I knew."

Listening carefully to the mother of this brain-injured infant, we realized that she was struggling with the loss of a much-yearned-for perfect baby. Other parents expressed this same feeling of having lost the baby that should have been theirs: "Every day I love him more, but I ache for that normal child." "You kind of let your fantasies fade—that normal child growing up, ballerina, kindergarten, grade school, college."

Anger and Frustration

Whether they found out at the birth or later on that their baby had a problem, all parents we spoke with described feelings of anger and frustration. Sometimes this anger was an overwhelming sensation directed at no one in particular. More frequently it was targeted at the doctor or the hospital. Sometimes the anger was directed at family or friends, and sometimes at their child.

"I'll never forget that morning in the hospital. This stupid intern strolled into the room and asked if I had seen my baby. Then, just like he was talking about the weather, he said, 'She may look a little funny to you, but she's going to be okay. It's just that she has a cleft palate.' "

The anger expressed by parents of handicapped infants has often been described as self-defense against anxiety and guilt. There are other plausible explanations. Many people, including physicians and nurses, do not feel comfortable with parents of a handicapped infant. Obstetricians, for instance, may feel that the birth of a handicapped baby is a challenge to their competence. Pediatricians, on the other hand, may feel uncomfortable about talking with parents because they have no good answers to the parents' questions. These feelings of inadequacy may interfere with the ability of medical personnel to be supportive with parents. Parents in turn are sensitive to this lack of sensitivity and respond with justified anger.

Similar dynamics may be in effect when anger is directed at friends and relations. A baby who is healthy and active, with a ready smile and a winning personality, makes friends for the parents. A baby who is irritable, sleepy, and unhealthy-looking makes people turn away. Parents interpret this reaction as rejection, not just of the baby, but of themselves.

"My friends, they were no help at all. One woman said right to my face, 'I'm sorry about your baby.' Like he died or got some horrible disease."

When parents turned their anger toward their baby, feelings of frustration mingled with the anger: "I went to a support group meeting for mothers of babies with Down syndrome. All these women kept talking about how great it was to have a Down syndrome baby. I had to leave. I couldn't deal with it. I figured there was something wrong with me thinking all the time that it would be best if my baby had died."

Feelings of anger toward the baby are as common as feelings of anger toward friends and family members. A baby with a problem is often irritable, demanding, and difficult to soothe. The baby may not respond to the mother's efforts to comfort him or may turn away from stimulation as if rejecting the mother. Parents of an unresponsive baby feel inadequate and unwanted, and these feelings can turn into anger at the baby. Parents who are already tired, upset, and frazzled may react to the baby's fussiness by losing control.

"I spent all my time crying and hating her. It would have helped to have someone say that they felt that way, too. I wouldn't have felt so guilty."

"In the beginning, every day was terrible and every night was worse. One night I literally walked the floor for three hours straight and she was still screeching—that horrible, high-pitched, grating kind of screech. I finally told her to shut her mouth, and I practically flung her into the crib. Thank God for my husband. He came in the room and told me calmly to go to bed, and he took over with the baby."

Depression, Fear, and Loneliness

Parents had little difficulty describing their feelings of anger, but they found sadness and fear more difficult to address. Most said they were initially overwhelmed by these painful emotions, but were able to resolve them and move on: "I cried every day of the first week, then every other day, then once a month. Now I cry about the same things as any other mother with a normal child would cry about."

"Fright, that's one feeling I had. I was really scared. I didn't know exactly what Down syndrome was. All I could think of was the retarded people that you feel sorry for in the store. I thought that there was no way I could raise my son, because I'd feel sorry for him just like I feel sorry for those people when I see them in the store."

A more subtle and perhaps more pervasive feeling that we identified in our interviews was a sense of vulnerability. Parents talked about how certain they had been that bad things couldn't happen to them.

"Other people have babies with encephalitis and cerebral palsy and spina bifida. *My* baby was going to be perfect, just the way everything else in my life had always been perfect. When the doctor told us about the spina bifida, I just couldn't believe it. Now I feel like I'm nude. Anything bad could happen to me."

"I'm not so much of a churchgoer, but I always believed that if you lived a good life, and you cared about other people, God would take care of you. For the first time in my life I look up at the stars and I question."

Depression, vulnerability, and loneliness, like anger, are described in the literature as a natural part of the adjustment process. Although this is a reasonable and well-supported interpretation, characterizing such feelings as a passing phase may be misleading. Mothers of older handicapped children talk about these emotions recurring. "Every time there is a transition like kindergarten, Sunday school, or Special Olympics, the fear and depression come back. I am up against a reality that I'll never be able to change."

Guilt and Self-Blame

Of all the feelings that parents described, guilt and self-blame were the most pervasive and the most difficult to overcome.

"I was angry with everyone—the doctor, the hospital, the candy-striper pushing the library cart—but most of all I was angry with myself. I should have been more careful during my pregnancy. People told me to take it easy, but I felt good and I just kept going full steam. Then all of a sudden I got toxemia, they did a C-section, and the baby's lungs weren't developed. Now who knows what kind of life this baby is going to have? If I could only turn the clock backwards!"

"I kept going over and over my pregnancy in my mind. I knew I had been very careful about what I ate—I didn't drink or smoke or take medicine or anything—but maybe there was something else. Then I'd get these really crazy thoughts that maybe I was being punished because I wanted this baby to be so perfect."

Guilt and self-blame are both common and maladaptive. The problem is that parents who engage in self-blaming can always find a tiny thread of truth. Maybe they did drink a little coffee or alcohol during their pregnancy. But it wasn't the cause of the problem. And even if they were in some part responsible for the problem, there is nothing to do about it. Feeling guilty will not make it better. When parents have difficulty handling these feelings, talking to a counselor may be helpful.

Reconciliation

No matter how much time parents spent describing their painful experiences, each wanted to tell us about the good times. Despite their conflicting feelings, they felt a real love for their child, and they wanted us to know how much pleasure the baby had brought to the family: "The deep hurt is there, the worrying about the future, the concerns about what will happen if something happens to us. But that is not what we think about most of the time. Most of the time we just enjoy her. It seems as if every day she is learning something new or doing something adorable. You know what she did the other day? Dennis came into the room wearing his cowboy hat, and she took the empty cereal bowl and stuck it on her head."

For most, a good support system and the absence of other life stressors made the adjustment easier. A less obvious but equally important factor was the growing love between parents and baby.

Impact of the Diagnosis

Parents who found out immediately that their baby was disabled seemed to be less traumatized than parents who found out later. They described the first disclosure as a bad moment, not a continuing trauma.

Falling in Love with Your Baby

When we asked parents who was most responsible for getting them out of their depression, the most frequent answer was the baby. Parents described antics that made them laugh, moments that made them proud, and interactions that made them feel needed and loved. As they talked about fun times with their child there was a dramatic change in mood: "Donna may not be an Einstein, but she sure can hold her own. The other day she counted up to five and her sister said, 'Bet you can't do it backwards.' You know what she did? She turned her back to her sister and counted to five again."

As parents talked about the pleasures they were getting from their baby, we realized that the literature describing the natural cycle of mourning does not tell the whole story. It is not just that parents go through a series of

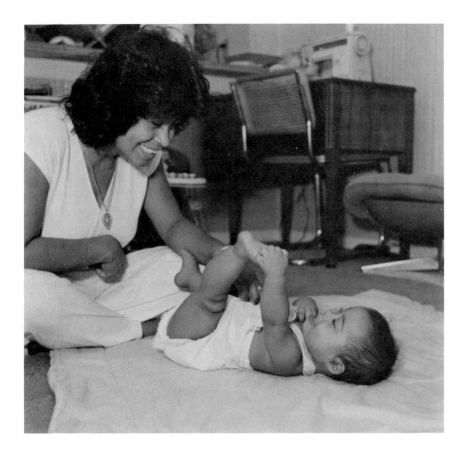

predictable stages and end up accepting their baby. The baby from the beginning plays a vital and dynamic role. As parents learn to interpret their baby's cues and respond to their baby's needs, the baby becomes more responsive and rewarding to his or her parents. Feelings of pain and anguish do not always disappear, but with time and love feelings of joy prevail.

CHAPTER

2

Marriage Under Stress

"Betty has been different since Jeffrey was born. She's only half there most of the time—like I can't really talk to her about anything. I guess she thinks I'm insensitive, but you can't spend your whole life in a blue funk."

No matter how strong the relationship with your spouse, a baby born with a problem can put a strain on your marriage. As you and your spouse deal with your separate fears and guilt, you may be uncommunicative when you need each other most.

In this chapter we explore ways couples relate to each other as they face the reality of parenting a handicapped child. We are concerned with the kinds of conflicts that occur, the differences in perspective that underlie these conflicts, and the kinds of compromises and resolutions that enable husband and wife to maintain a supportive relationship.

When Mothers and Fathers Are Out of Step

As we talked to couples about their baby's disability, we found out that many husbands and wives disagree with each other when they talk about their baby's problem. This is particularly true when the baby shows signs of developmental delay but has not been diagnosed as handicapped. In these situations mothers, who often have closer daily contact with the child, were usually first to suspect the problem. Some of the husbands we spoke with made light of their wives' concern.

> Husband: "What do you expect? He's only a baby. He should recite the Gettysburg Address?"
>
> Wife: "You know what I expect. He's a year old and he should be making sounds. Pretending there isn't a problem isn't going to help."

In situations where either the husband or the wife continued to deny the problem, heated arguments were inevitable. Some couples tried to avoid these arguments by agreeing not to talk about the baby. This lack of communication augmented their fears, and they reached out to others for support: "I'm so thankful that I found Ring-A-Round. For a man with 20-20 vision, my husband is blind as a bat. He's made up his mind that there's nothing wrong with the baby and that I'm just being neurotic."

Philosophic Differences

In many situations parents are able to agree on the nature of a problem but disagree violently on how to manage it. One spouse may believe strongly in letting nature take its course, while the other tries to speed up development through nonstop infant stimulation: "My wife drives herself and the baby crazy. All he wants to do is sleep, and there she is shaking the rattle and squeaking that darn rubber duck."

Another area of philosophic difference is child management. Disagreements can arise over any aspect of child care. Should the baby be allowed to cry? Can the baby be left with a sitter? Should the baby be put to sleep in the family bed? When parents are already tired and tense, minor disagreements turn into major battles: "Handicapped or not handicapped, I don't want Alicia to turn into a spoiled brat. The way my husband gives in to her every whim, we're going to have a monster on our hands!"

Self-sacrifice

Even when couples are in agreement about how to parent, a baby with a handicap can jeopardize a marriage. In some situations one parent, often the mother, has to stop working in order to take care of the baby. The nonworking parent may feel angry about being left at home. The working parent may feel overwhelmed by the burden of being the sole financial support of the family. Although couples may recognize that they have worked out the only plausible compromise, feelings of resentment can persist.

An even greater threat to a marriage may be overzealousness. When one or both parents make a conscious decision to devote their whole life to the baby, the marriage has to suffer: "When we found out that Jerod was deaf, we made a pledge on the spot. No matter what we had to do, no matter how much we had to sacrifice, we would do everything in our power to make life easier for Jerod."

Parents who devote their lives to their baby are always in danger of devoting too little time to each other. This is particularly true when the time commitment of the couple is uneven, with one parent taking on most of the child-care responsibility. Tensions between husband and wife can begin to feed on themselves. Disagreements turn into resentment, and couples who need each other very badly find themselves drifting apart.

Nurturing Your Marriage

Recognizing that having a child with a problem adds stress to marriage, parents need to seek ways of nurturing their relationship. The following suggestions come from parents who have been through tough times and have come out with their marriages intact:

Find time on a regular basis to be alone with your spouse. The extra stimulation you may have provided your baby or the tears you may have prevented are not as important as your marriage. If the problem is finding a baby-sitter, make it a top priority and don't be too proud to ask favors of friends.

Set side time for yourself on a daily basis. Read a magazine, go for a walk, listen to music, engage in a sport, or visit a friend. Every human being, no matter how strong or energetic, needs time for self-renewal. The better you take care of yourself, the more you will be available to your baby and your spouse.

Talk to each other about your feelings and try to understand each other's point of view. Perhaps your spouse resents the amount of time you are devoting to the baby, or perhaps he or she feels you are spoiling the baby by being at her beck and call. Perhaps your spouse feels that you are not taking your share of responsibility with the baby or that you don't recognize how needy the baby is. When you make a special effort to understand each other's point of view, it is easier to come up with some reasonable compromises.

Avoid sending double messages. Parents of handicapped children often ask for help and then criticize the helper. Perhaps your partner can't change

a diaper as quickly as you can or hasn't got the knack of getting up the burp. If you find yourself hovering over your spouse to make sure he or she does everything right, it may be a good idea to leave the room. Your partner's involvement is important for you and your baby, and a little bit of awkward handling is not going to hurt your child.

Do not pretend with each other. Share your bad feelings as well as your good ones. All parents have moments when they look back longingly to the days before the baby was born, when they were free of worry and responsibility. It's all right to say out loud that sometimes you resent the baby. When husband and wife give voice to their bad feelings, they become more supportive of each other.

Spend time together enjoying your baby without worrying about therapy. Silly, playful moments are tonic for the whole family.

CHAPTER

3

Grandparents' Role

Part of the joy of childbirth and child rearing is sharing the new baby with close friends and family. Grandparents can be especially important. Their expressions of delight as they admire their new grandchild enhance the celebration. Even couples who distanced themselves from their parents as they cemented their own marriage may sense a new camaraderie. Tensions and conflicts are set aside as the baby takes center stage.

When there is a problem with the baby, the joy is mixed with tension and concern. Grandparents and the new parents may have difficulty sharing their feelings. Perhaps they try to hide their feelings in order to protect each other. Perhaps they express their anxiety in ways that are hurtful.

In this chapter we examine the kinds of rifts that can occur when communication breaks down between grandparents and new parents. We also look at situations where grandparents have been especially supportive and have seen their children through the roughest periods. In the final section we explore ways grandparents and their children can reach out to each other and establish a mutually supportive relationship.

Mothers and Grandmothers

Many mothers find it difficult to break the news to their mothers. A new mother may want to protect her mother or avoid a painful subject. She may want to spare herself the pain of seeing her mother hurt: "The hardest part of this whole thing was telling my mother. She had been so excited about this baby. When I finally told her, she put up a real brave front. She put her hand on my arm and said in this cheerful voice, 'Well, it's a tough break, but we've had tough breaks before and we always come out on top.' And then her mascara started to run, and I know she was fighting back tears."

In some situations it is the grandmother who guesses that there may be a problem with the baby and tries to protect the mother. Often the best of intentions backfire, and her probing of the doctors for information is interpreted as interference: "My mother is giving me a hard time. She's trying to find out more about the problem and keeps looking for something worse. She never tells me directly, but I know what she's up to."

When mother and daughter have difficulty communicating openly about a handicapped child, it can usually be traced to long-standing conflicts. Often, both mother and daughter fantasize that sharing a new grandchild will put an end to their conflicts and mark a turning point in their relationship. Grandparents expect their children to be less judgmental when they discover firsthand what it is like to parent. Daughters expect to be treated as equals as they step into the parent role. Unfortunately, the birth of a handicapped child is likely to increase, rather than decrease, existing tensions. Old issues, like sibling rivalry, struggles with separation, and conflicts over autonomy appear once again.

"My mother practically lives in my kitchen, and she's always there with an opinion. 'You spend too much time with that baby. You'll spoil him to death. Why don't you let him cry? It's good for his lungs. Shouldn't he be wearing a warmer outfit? It's freezing in this house. I don't want to interfere or anything, but shouldn't you be giving him vitamins?' "

Yet establishment of a new mutually supportive mother-daughter relationship is not impossible: "We used to fight all the time, but things are better now. At least we can talk about things. I'm glad about it, because I know that Katherine needs all the love and support she can get."

If you feel your parents have overstepped their boundaries, discuss the problem openly. It is natural for parents who have always shouldered responsibility for their children to continue in that role. It is up to you to explain that, although you need and appreciate their love and support, you are in charge of your baby.

If you think your parents are not spending enough time with their grandchild or are not helping out enough, discuss that too. Perhaps your parents are trying so hard not to interfere that they don't realize how welcome they are.

Help your parents feel comfortable about taking care of the baby. It is natural for grandparents to lose their confidence if they believe the baby is fragile. With a little practice and guidance, they will learn to trust themselves with the baby.

Give your parents very clear messages. Don't just hint that you would like some financial help or that you need them to do more baby-sitting. It is much easier on everyone if you make your needs explicit.

If grandparents are reluctant to baby-sit, do not take it as a rejection of your baby. Perhaps your parents don't like to go out at night, or perhaps they are nervous about the responsibility of taking care of the baby. Talk about it openly. Your parents may be more comfortable if you bring the child to their house, or they may volunteer to pay for a baby-sitting service.

Find specific ways to involve grandparents in taking care of the baby. Try teaching them how to play a language game or showing them how to exercise the baby. This active involvement builds your parents' confidence, gives you an extra pair of hands, and creates a closer bond between grandparent and grandchild.

If you have tried everything with your parents and nothing seems to work, give it time. Just as your children have a way of making you love them, grandchildren have a knack for winning over their grandparents.

Suggestions for Grandparents

No matter how right you know you are, don't criticize your children for what they did in the past. It won't change anything.

Talk openly with your children. If you are concerned about asking too many questions, share your concern with your children: "Matthew is very special to me. I want to know as much as you feel comfortable telling me. I don't want you to feel as if you have to protect me."

Let your children know that you understand what they are going through. A sympathetic word goes a long way.

If you are uncomfortable about handling the baby, be honest with your children and let them know this. You can find other ways of being supportive until you feel ready.

Enforce the behavioral limits that are set for your grandchild. If the parents have said, "No candy," don't give the child one little piece. Don't ever be tempted to give in to a child because he has a handicap.

Don't be a Pollyanna. Assuring parents that their child will outgrow the problem makes facing up to the problem more difficult.

In this chapter we have made some suggestions to ease the tensions and improve communication between grandparents and parents. Remember, a technique that works beautifully for one family can be a disaster for another. Each family brings its own mixture of understanding, caring, education, social customs, emotional stability, and a host of other characteristics. How these mesh will probably determine what kind of relationship is possible. Our advice is to read about the experiences of other families and the resolutions they have reached and select those ideas that may be helpful for your family.

CHAPTER

4

Siblings

"Tony is one of those really happy-go-lucky, good-natured children. He is unbelievably patient with his little sister, who has cerebral palsy. He lets her walk all over him. One day Tony had a fever, and we decided to take him to the doctor. He put up such a fuss you wouldn't believe it. Finally he asked us in this really scared voice, 'Is the doctor going to say I catched cerebal palsy?' "

Children seem to have a sixth sense. Even when parents are careful not to have disturbing discussions in front of them, they know their parents are concerned about the new baby. Sometimes children react to their parents' concern by developing secret fears. Maybe the baby is going to die, and everyone will get sad. Maybe cerebral palsy is catching, and they are going to get sick.

In this chapter we discuss how a handicapped child affects the dynamics of the family. We explore the impact of a handicapped child on older and younger siblings and describe positive and negative sibling reactions. Finally, we suggest ways parents can help their nonhandicapped children deal with the problems and reap the rewards of having a handicapped sibling.

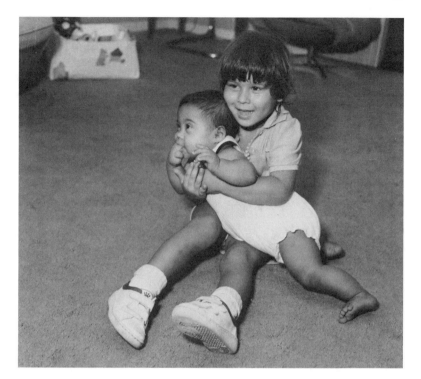

Secret Fears

Parents are often surprised when their nonhandicapped child expresses an irrational fear associated with the baby's handicap. When Tony talked about catching cerebral palsy, his mother's first reaction was to laugh at such a silly idea. When you think about it, however, you really can't expect a four-year-old to make the distinction between the condition a child is born with and the diseases that are contagious.

While some of the secret fears that siblings harbor can be attributed to a lack of information, their most haunting fears may reflect a sensitivity to nonverbal communication. When parents are worried and upset about the baby, the other siblings sense it. Often, children are too afraid to ask questions, so parents become convinced that they have protected their children from worry.

Jealousy

In families with more than one child, a certain amount of jealousy is inevitable. It is certainly not surprising to find jealousy intensified in families with a special needs child. Children discover at an early age that expressing jealousy about a handicapped sibling is not acceptable. A child's logical solution is often to get his or her share of attention by helping with the baby. As siblings fuss over the baby, they gain center stage as mother's or father's little helper.

Another strategy for gaining attention is to imitate the baby. Older siblings cling, whine, and act like a baby, or develop an array of symptoms that provoke a sympathetic response. Recognizing the reasons for their behavior, parents often go overboard to give the older child a fair share of attention. Unfortunately, too much attention to imaginary illnesses can make matters worse. Children and parents find it increasingly difficult to distinguish between real and imagined complaints.

A third strategy for gaining attention in a preoccupied family is to act out. Young children discover that breaking a lamp, spilling a glass of orange juice on the floor, or grabbing the rattle out of the baby's hands gets them attention, even if it is negative. Children are often very up front about their jealous feelings: "That's why I broked it, 'cause I'm mad. Tim gets all the presents, and he don't do nothing good. He cries and he spits and he poops in his diaper and he stinks!"

When children use these strategies to gain their share of attention, parents have little trouble reading and responding to their cues. The children who appear to show no resentment or jealousy are the ones who need closer watching. Occasionally the sibling of a handicapped child accepts the situation and makes no demands at all. These children may be undervaluing themselves. They may believe that because they do not have a handicap they are not very important and can make no demands: "Mommy can't come to school to see our play. She's got to watch my brother. He's got zebra palsy."

Quiet, compliant behavior becomes a way of coping—but, like boisterous behavior, it is simply an attempt to cover up hurt.

Children who grow up with a handicapped older sibling have less difficulty with adjustment than older siblings. Very often the older handicapped child becomes a playmate for the younger child, and a healthy friendship develops. In this situation sibling problems may be kept to a minimum. The following kind of exchange has probably occurred in many families:

"Mom, can I bring Angela to Terry's birthday party?"

"Did you ask Terry if it's all right?"

"He won't mind, 'cause she's my sister."

Handling Teasing

Brother: "Jeremy says that Susan is an idiot."

Mother: "That must have made you feel angry."

Brother: "Yeah, that made me mad. What's an idiot?"

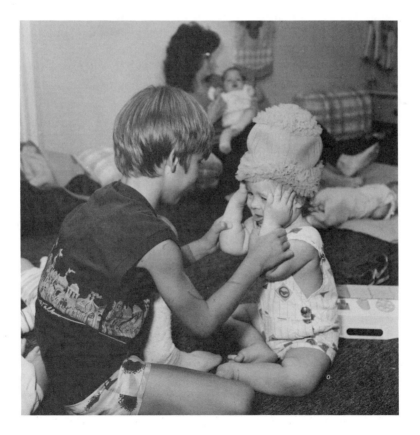

Parents with a handicapped child are always concerned when their children are teased about their sibling. Sometimes children are ostracized by the neighbors because they have a funny-looking brother or sister. Fortunately, in recent years, through the efforts of the media and the schools, people are becoming more knowledgeable about handicapping conditions; families with a handicapped child are less likely to be stigmatized. Although we may hear about a child from time to time who has had to defend a handicapped sibling, it is seldom a major problem.

Balancing Attention

Some of the problems that siblings of handicapped babies experience are not related directly to their sibling's special needs. In some families parents shower too much attention on their *nonhandicapped* child. Some families overindulge their nonhandicapped children to shield them from the insensitivities they may have to face. Other families may put too much pressure on the nonhandicapped child, making him or her the focus of all their hopes and dreams. No child is perfect, and living up to unrealistic expectations can be a heavy burden. The nonhandicapped sibling may become too grown-up, too studious, or too responsible. The end product could be an overanxious child who hasn't learned the art of having fun.

We have talked so far about the negatives of having a handicapped sibling. But there is a flip side. Children with a handicapped sibling are likely to feel confident, successful, and good about themselves. They develop a special talent for playing with their handicapped sibling, which delights their parents and earns them genuine praise. Their interaction with a handicapped sibling makes them sensitive and empathetic, and they have little trouble making friends. Finally, parents who live with a handicapped child are tuned in to the special accomplishments of their nonhandicapped child and boost their child's self-confidence.

Suggestions for Parents

Although most studies show that siblings of handicapped children fare very well in the long run, it is important for parents to help their children

cope with some of the inevitable problems and avoid unnecessary hurt.

Tell your child about the baby's problem in a matter-of-fact way and in words he can understand. "Jeremy is a baby with Down syndrome. This means that he will walk, talk, and learn new things more slowly than other children. Down syndrome is something you are born with, like some people are born with red hair. It is not something that you catch."

"Alicia has cerebral palsy. The part of her brain that tells her arms and legs what to do doesn't work very well. Alicia is going to have trouble learning to walk and may have to use crutches or a wheelchair. She's lucky to have a big brother to help her learn to use crutches or push her around in the wheelchair."

"Tarren is hearing impaired. Something went wrong before she was born, and she can't hear noises or voices the way you and I can. The hearing aids we put on her will help her learn to hear a little bit. Because Tarren has trouble hearing people talk to her, it will take a long time for her to learn to talk. You and I will have to be very patient when we try to help her talk."

Help your child find words to describe her negative feelings. "You're feeling angry with your baby brother. He does a lot of crying, and he takes up so much of our time." "You felt sad today when your friends made fun of Eric. People sometimes make fun of things that they don't understand. Maybe one day you can invite your friends over and we'll tell them about cerebral palsy."

If your child shares her feelings spontaneously, be a good listener. Accept her feelings without being judgmental and adding to her resentment.

> "I hate her, I hate her, I hate her and I wish she never got borned. Now we can't even go to Grandma's house 'cause she went and got sick."
>
> "You really feel awful about not going to Grandma's house. Too bad Susie is running a fever."

> "Andrew is going to die, and then you and Mom are going to die and leave me all alone."
>
> "It's scary when Andrew gets sick and we have to take him to the hospital. I'm glad he's feeling better. You know, your mom and I are not going to die for a very long time, and we will never leave you alone."

Set aside a special time every day to spend with each of your children, even if it's only five minutes. Tell your children how important this special time is to you: "Our baby keeps us busy. But I'm glad we have this special time for me and you to be together."

Avoid making your children feel guilty. Instead of saying, "You're selfish to eat that cookie in front of your brother," say, "Eat your cookie in the other room so Paul won't see it."

Instead of saying, "Don't make your sister sick by kissing her when you have a runny nose," say, "You have a runny nose. You better not kiss your sister."

Read your child books about handicapped children. A sensitively written book can help a child understand and empathize with their handicapped sibling. Look for books that describe the reactions of siblings to their handicapped brother or sister. It will help your child realize that other children have felt jealous, left out, and resentful. A list of books is presented in the Appendix.

If your nonhandicapped child is between three and six years old, you may want to try role-playing. Give your child an opportunity to pretend to be handicapped. You can alternate between staying in the role of parent or taking the part of the nonhandicapped sibling. You could also play out the same dynamics by using a playhouse family.

Encourage your nonhandicapped children to invite friends to the house. Make sure your child introduces her friends to her handicapped sibling. Help your child learn simple ways to answer the questions their friends might ask.

"Why does your sister make those awful noises?"

"She can't hear the sounds she makes, so she doesn't know they're awful."

"Why does your sister drool all the time?"

"She has trouble learning to swallow her spit. We're teaching her how to wipe her mouth with a tissue."

"How come your brother doesn't know how to sit up?"

"He doesn't learn to do things as fast as other babies. We don't know why."

CHAPTER

5

Changing Friendships

"I don't know what's the matter with Robin. I met her at the dentist's, and she acted very cold. Like she didn't even know me. She had her baby with her. I think he may have Down syndrome. And when I started to talk to him she whisked him away, saying she was in a hurry."

When a couple has a handicapped baby, particularly if it is a first child, established friendship patterns are likely to change. Some of the reasons for this change are obvious. Admittedly, time is a factor. Free time is at a premium, and finding a sitter with enough experience to care for a handicapped child is not easy. When there is time for socialization, it is natural for couples to gravitate toward other families who have similar problems.

Couples who keep in touch with old friends agree it takes special effort. The first encounter is always the most difficult. Inevitably the old friends ask about the baby, and it's hard to know how much to tell. Do they really want to know about the delivery, or are they making polite conversation? It takes time for couples to break down their defenses and talk comfortably with each other.

If the old friends are already parents, the renewal of the friendship may

be particularly difficult. Couples may find themselves in an approach-avoidance conflict. On one hand they really want to visit with their friends and talk about old times. On the other hand, they are concerned about seeing a baby who is developmentally on target and bound to outperform their baby. A father described his reactions to a visit from his college roommate.

"I was glad to see them, but at the same time it was a shock. I never really believed that Samantha was behind until we spent some time with Joey. That kid was all over the place, digging up the house plants, climbing on the furniture, splashing the water in the toilets. It's not that we cared about the mess he was making. It's just that it hurt so much to watch Samantha just sit there, unable to move."

Whether or not your friends have children, you may feel uncomfortable about reestablishing the friendship. The experience of having a handicapped child can play havoc with your self-confidence, and you may think of yourself as socially unattractive.

"My wife and I lived like hermits for a while. Frankly, we were embarrassed about having a funny-looking kid with a big head. No, it was more than that, we felt inadequate and disgraced. I know it doesn't make sense, but that's the way we felt. And then a funny thing happened. A neighbor came to the house and started playing with our kid. Jeffrey started laughing and then we started laughing, and from that moment on things started getting better."

After the ice is broken, most couples report that keeping up with friendships has been an important part of getting their lives back in order. As their friends get to know their baby, talking gets easier and they regain their confidence.

Even when parents get over the hurdle of socializing with their friends, taking the baby out in public may be difficult. Parents often tell stories about insensitive strangers who ask impertinent questions or give unsolicited advice. ("Is your baby a Mongoloid? You know you could get him operated on. I saw it on TV.") But most of the strangers who come up to the stroller are simply attracted to babies. If they ask how old the baby is, they are probably making conversation and not checking out developmental milestones.

As a defense against questions that make them feel uncomfortable, parents can develop some pat answers that discourage further questions without creating embarrassment.

> "That baby looks like he's too big to carry."
> "He is getting big. I'll be glad when he learns to walk."
>
> "Your baby looks like she's going to fall asleep any second."
> "Yes, she does look sleepy."
>
> "Is your baby a Mongoloid?"
> "She has Down syndrome."

Even when parents have overcome their "stranger anxiety," they may find themselves becoming less social and more reclusive. Laughter can be jarring when you are worried or depressed, and putting up a good front when you are feeling down is not always easy to do. While some reclusiveness is natural during the adjustment period, it is important not to make it a habit. For the sake of your child as well as the rest of the family, try to keep yourself in the mainstream, inviting social encounters and enlarging your circle of friends.

When parents are ready to reach out and make new friends, the most accessible prospects may be parents with disabled babies. These are the

people who are most likely to understand how you feel and to share your joys and concerns. Unfortunately, despite the availability of already established support groups, many parents have difficulty taking the first step. You may perceive the decision to join a support group as a confirmation of your baby's handicap and as an abandonment of hope. Even when parents do decide to join a parents' group, it may take them awhile to find a group that really meets their needs.

"It wasn't easy for me to join Ring-A-Round. When I first saw all those babies with handicaps sitting around in a circle, I wanted to run away. My son wasn't going to be like that. He was developmentally delayed, and he would outgrow his problem. But then when a parent urged me to come into the room, I saw my son's reaction. He was clapping his hands to the music and having a wonderful time. Pretty soon I heard myself saying that next week I'd bring the snack."

One of the major benefits of joining a parent support group is the opportunity you gain to give as well as receive support. As you reach out to help another parent, you will reinforce your own coping skills. At the same time, your baby will have the opportunity to be with other children.

PART II

EVERYDAY LIVING

"I feel uncomfortable when I'm away from Brett. I know he's just a baby and he'll be fine without me, but somehow I feel that no one can take care of him quite as well as I can. I know by the sound of his breathing and the way he moves that he's going to awaken, and I lift him out of the crib before he starts to cry. I know just how to hold him, cradle, rock, and soothe him, and get him back to sleep. It's as if I'm part of him and he's part of me."

In Part I we talked about the feelings that parents work through as they adjust to the reality of their baby's problems. In this section the major focus is on the baby. We see how parents stay in touch with their infants, recognizing their special characteristics and responding to their individual needs.

Chapter 6, "Reading Your Baby's Cues," describes the different ways infants express their needs. We examine the different ways babies signal their need for stimulation or their need for quiet time. We also look at built-in temperamental differences and discuss ways to adapt your care-giving style to fit your baby's temperament.

In Chapter 7, "Day-to-day Care," the focus is on the routines of daily living. We discuss common problems that emerge around feeding, dressing, bathing, and putting the baby to sleep and provide practical suggestions to overcome these problems.

In Chapter 8, "Discipline and Social Skills," we identify ways to help toddlers develop social skills, accept limitations, and control impulsive behavior.

CHAPTER

6

Reading Your
Baby's Cues

Every child comes into the world helpless and alone. The baby's survival depends on his ability to make his needs known and to invoke care-giving behaviors. During the early years, the connections that the baby makes with parents or care-givers are his lifeline. They are the baby's way of rising out of helplessness and developing an awareness of self and a sense of security, control, and purpose.

Just as your baby is affected by the quality of care-giving he receives, your baby is affecting you by the quality of his responses. The infant who cries when hungry and calms down when fed has initiated an unspoken dialogue: "I need, you respond, and I'm comforted."

A critical task of the infant is to signal his needs to his care-giver. A critical task for the care-giver is to interpret and respond to these needs. As the signal-and-response system takes hold in infancy, infant and parent are tuned into each other, and a love bond is cemented. In infants at risk, where the cues are indistinct, hard to read, and often confusing, the bonding process may be slower. For a while you may feel inadequate as you struggle to interpret those muted cues. In the long run, the energy and the effort expanded by infant and parent can make bonding all the stronger.

In this chapter we explore the ways you come to know your baby, by reading and responding to subtle behavioral cues. First we look at natural

fluctuations in behavior, recognizing that every baby has times during the day when he is quiet and alert, times when he is drowsy, and times when he is agitated. Second, we examine differences in temperament, activity level, sensitivity to stimuli, adaptability, and quality of mood. Finally we suggest ways you can recognize and respond to your baby's cues and signals.

States of Awareness

As your newborn baby awakens from sleep or goes from wakeful attentiveness to agitated crying, you will recognize the various states of her sleeping/waking cycles. Experts call these different ways of responding to stimuli the baby's state of arousal. Different parts of the brain control the different stages of your baby's behavior.

1. In deep sleep, the baby is sleeping quietly. Her breathing is regular, and there are no visible eye movements.

2. In wakeful or REM sleep the baby is asleep but restless. REM stands for rapid eye movements, because the baby's eyes can be seen moving back and forth under her almost-closed lids. Her breathing is likely to be irregular.

3. In the drowsy state the baby is awake but inattentive. Her eyes look glazed and unfocused.

4. In the state of quiet alertness, the baby's eyes are focused. She looks interested and aware and is ready to take in new information.

5. In the state of active wakefulness, the baby is less focused. Some babies will kick and wave their arms. Others will stiffen, squirm, and begin to fuss.

6. In the state of crying, the baby's face is distorted. Her eyes may be open or tightly closed.

Babies who have well-established sleep/wake cycles move from one state to the next in a smooth and predictable way. The baby who is in a quiet alert state, for instance, may be going up the cycle, increasing her activity level until she reaches crying, or down the cycle into drowsiness and sleep. Babies who are premature or immature at birth may take several months to establish these six distinctive states.

As your baby's states become distinct enough to identify, you will want to maximize the amount of time that your baby is quiet and alert. You can bring your baby up from a state of drowsiness to a state of quiet alertness by introducing the right amount of stimulation. You will also find ways of quieting your baby when she is crying or active in order to bring her back down to a state of quiet alertness.

When a baby is either actively crying or looking drowsy and half-awake, it is natural to assume that the baby should be comforted and put to sleep. In actuality, a drowsy baby may be in the process of awakening, and a crying baby may be ready for some active playtime. If your baby is drowsy but appears to be awakening, approach the crib talking in a soft but high-pitched voice, and see if your baby responds by making eye contact. If your baby is crying or fussy but not hungry, cradle her in your arms or place her in a bounce chair. Talk to her softly, making sure that she can see your face and watch your lips move. She may enjoy some "conversation" before she falls asleep. Changes in the loudness and pitch of your voice as you talk to your baby should occur gradually to avoid startling her.

Temperamental Differences

Since the early 1960s, researchers have tried to identify individual differences present at birth that have significance for later development. The task has not been easy. Infants change very rapidly, and behaviors that characterize an infant one day may be gone the next. Also, babies are sensitive to care-givers, and both the significance and the predictability of a characteristic are related to the care-giving environment. At the same time, an infant who is irritable at birth may be experiencing a physiologic adjustment, becoming accustomed to living in the world outside the warm surroundings of his mother's uterus. If the mother interprets the infant's behavior as signaling a permanent characteristic or as a reflection of her own inexperience, her negative reactions could stabilize the trait.

To identify temperamental characteristics that are present at birth and stable over time, researchers have followed the same babies through their growing-up period. They have scrutinized the individual differences present at birth as well as parenting styles and characteristics. Through these studies, they have been able to identify dimensions of difference in infancy that affect care-giving needs. They have also recognized clusters of characteristics that make it easier or more difficult to parent a newborn child.

Babies who from the start are placid and easy to soothe, who adapt easily to new situations, who are predictable in terms of sleeping and eating, and who are neither too easy nor too difficult to arouse are thought of as "easy babies." Babies who are sluggish, difficult to arouse, disturbed by new stimuli, and irritable, or babies who are active, irregular, easily aroused, and hard to soothe are considered to be "difficult babies." Unfortunately, many of the characteristics that are associated with a difficult temperament are also associated with babies who have physical disabilities.

Easy Babies

An easy baby makes life easy for his parents. The easy baby can be thought of as "forgiving." If the parent takes a long time to get the bottle ready, the baby tolerates the wait. If the parents decide to visit a friend, the baby is content to go to sleep in a strange place. The baby does a lot of smiling and little crying, giving parents the unspoken message, "You are doing fine." The baby is a joy to hold and cuddle, and his pleasant behavior is reinforced.

Preterm babies or babies who have a difficult beginning may have some, but not all, of the characteristics of an easy baby. They may spend a lot of time sleeping and fall back to sleep with no difficulty after a period of wakefulness. Unlike easy babies, they spend little time in the beginning in a state of quiet alertness. Parents have the special challenge of providing modulated stimulation that engages their baby's attention and helps him achieve a quiet alert state.

- Stroke your baby softly on the cheek or play gently with his fingers and toes.

- Sing or chant a lullaby or ring a small bell with a pleasant tinkle.

- Swing or rock your baby, slowly and easily, in an infant seat.

- Show your baby a colorful ribbon or scarf.

If your baby responds to modulated stimulation without showing signs of overload, increase the stimulation gradually. You may want to sing quietly as you wave the ribbon or bounce the infant seat with a little more vigor. Babies who respond well to modulated stimulation do not usually like sudden changes in activities or changes in the intensity of the stimuli.

Difficult Babies

When a baby is born with a difficult temperament, the role of the parent, particularly in the first year, is much more challenging. If the baby is easily aroused by stimuli such as light, sound, and touch, he will be disturbed by a mild increase in stimulation. The slightest noise will startle him, a room full of people may set off a panicked cry, or he may be oblivious to the noise of the crowd. If a baby is temperamentally slow to

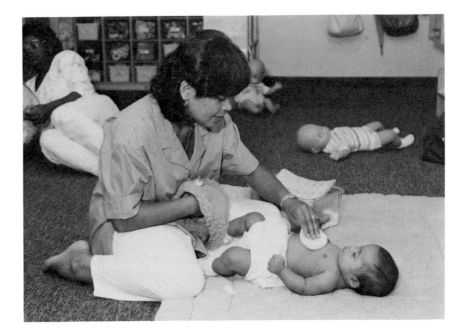

warm up, he may react negatively to any kind of change or new experience. The first bath may be a disaster, and changing the blanket on his crib may provoke a bedtime crisis. Babies who tend to be irritable or hard to soothe may respond to being handled with louder cries or by extending their arms and legs. Parents may feel rejected.

Babies who are easily aroused or hyperalert are also likely to be slow to warm up. These babies require sensitive and caring parents who recognize how easily they are overloaded and seek out ways to modify and control the environment. Parents need to be alert to the particular kind of stimulation that is disturbing to their baby. Some babies are especially sensitive to noises, some to bright light, and some in changes in texture. Other babies may be upset by quick and jerky movements. When parents can anticipate the kinds of stimuli or changes in stimulation that their baby has difficulty with, they can introduce modifications that build up the baby's level of tolerance. The task becomes even more demanding when the baby responds inconsistently—rejecting being cuddled one day and enjoying it the next.

Although hypersensitive and slow-to-warm-up babies are not necessarily at risk, extreme hypersensitivity is usually associated with prematurity or a physical disability. Babies with cerebral palsy may be particularly sensitive to quick movement or sudden noises. A dropped rattle can make them startle or quiver. A blind or hearing-impaired baby may be upset by an unexpected touch or tickle.

If your baby is sensitive to bright lights, keep a night light on in his bedroom. When you need the room to be brighter, turn on a lamp with a low-wattage bulb. When your baby has adjusted to this amount of light, you can turn on an overhead light or a full-wattage lamp. Some parents find a light on a rheostat (dimmer switch) helpful.

If your baby is sensitive to noise, tone down those noises that are likely to disturb him. Turn the ring on your telephone to its lowest level and muffle a noisy doorbell. Talk to your baby in a soft voice and gradually raise the volume. If the problem persists, installing acoustical tile on the ceiling and using drapes are simple ways to help control extraneous noises.

If your baby is sensitive to texture, be careful about the sheets you put on his crib, the clothes you wear, and the clothes you dress him in. If he is used to a cotton sheet on his crib, buy another cotton sheet rather than a polyester one. Wash a new outfit before you put it on him to make sure it is soft enough. Let him touch it or play with it. Pay attention to the texture of your own clothes. If you are wearing a rough-textured shirt or sweater, you may want to slip on a housecoat before you begin his feeding.

If your baby is disturbed by new experiences, modify your daily routine so that any new experience is introduced slowly. The first time you give your baby a bath, let him watch you make the preparations. Be sure to choose a quiet time during the day so that he won't be bombarded with other kinds of stimulation. Place him on a towel or sponge in a baby tub with very little lukewarm water. Every few days increase the amount of water until his body is submerged. Talk to him gently as you bathe him to keep him calm and relaxed.

If your baby is difficult to soothe, try to identify and avoid situations that can upset your baby. Hard-to-soothe babies are often distressed by sudden changes in the amount of stimulation, or by an increased level of stimulation over a relatively long period of time. A room full of company that most babies can ignore or tune out might really upset a hard-to-soothe baby. No matter how hard you try to stay away from these stressful situations, there are times when they are unavoidable. There will also be times when your baby becomes agitated and frantic for no identifiable reason.

The best way to calm a hard-to-soothe baby is to reduce the amount of stimulation. It may be possible to bring your baby into a quiet room and

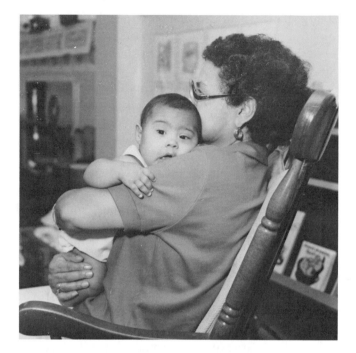

rock him gently. For some babies even this may not be enough; their own active thrashing in your arms may maintain their overload. When this happens put your baby down in the crib in a quiet, darkened room. Once he is down, talk to him softly, pat him gently and rhythmically, and cover him with a familiar blanket. When he has discharged his energy through active crying, he is likely to calm himself and fall quietly to sleep.

As parents adjust their own behavior in response to their baby's temperament, it is important to recognize that a baby's temperament is something he was born with and does not reflect their adequacy as parents. Hard-to-soothe babies or babies who are too easily aroused are not rejecting their parents. On the contrary, they are sending out a message that says, "I need your special kind of caring. I am easily overwhelmed."

Signals of Stress

Just as babies are born with a set of reflexes that have survival value, they also have distinct ways of signaling and reacting to stress. In the early months a baby will react with her whole body to any type of stress situation: a bright light, a loud noise, a sudden change in position, or an overstimulating care-giver. Parents become sensitized to the special ways their baby signals stress or overload, and either modify the environment or help their baby cope.

The ways babies signal stress are often very subtle: a change of expression, a tightening of the lips, a curling of the toes, or a slight change in color. Other stress signals include hiccupping, spitting up, turning dusky, or having a bowel movement. When your baby is showing signs of stress it is important, of course, first to reduce the amount of stimulation. Equally important is helping your baby organize her own resources and learn self-calming strategies. Sometimes putting your hand on your baby's stomach or back is enough to help her reorganize. At other times you may be able to give her a pacifier, or put her arms close to her body and her finger near her mouth.

Tuning in to your baby, recognizing her unique needs and special characteristics, and identifying ways to meet these needs is a never-ending challenge. Babies are capable of sudden spurts in development that modify their needs and change their capabilities. Often parents have to walk a tightrope. On one hand you want to be there for your baby, protecting her from discomfort. On the other hand you want your baby to learn self-regulation, coping, and adapting to changes in her environment.

CHAPTER

7

Day-to-Day Care

"Seven and a half pounds and our whole house is full of baby—diapers, cradles, carry-cribs, baby bottles in the sink, nighty-nights in the shower—and every one in the house at her beck and call."

A full-term and thriving newborn baby can place the household on active 24-hour duty, particularly in the first few weeks when the baby and the household are adjusting to each other. When the baby is born premature or at risk, the period of active 24-hour duty may continue for a very long time. The baby's erratic sleep and eating patterns make it difficult to establish a schedule, and parents find themselves chronically overtired. The calm and organized household that parents want so much for the baby is almost impossible to achieve.

This chapter focuses on the routines of daily living. We look at eating, sleeping, holding, changing, and other care-giving routines that take up a significant part of each day. In the second section we turn our attention to the toddler period and examine some typical problems associated with behavioral management.

Feeding

In the early months parents spend more time in feeding their baby than in any other care-giving activity. When feeding routines go smoothly, other routines are likely to follow suit. In most situations, however, parents do have some concerns associated with feeding their special needs baby.

When you have a choice between breast-feeding and bottle-feeding, most doctors agree that breast-feeding has nutritional advantages. Breast milk contains the appropriate ratio of carbohydrates to fats and proteins and a good supply of calcium and other minerals. It also provides immunity against certain infections. From the point of view of the mother it is usually easy, pleasant, and comfortable. Breast-feeding provides a special opportunity for the mother to feel close to her baby.

Despite the advantages of breast milk, mothers with handicapped babies are less likely to breast-feed than mothers with normally developing babies. There are several reasons for this, including problems with sucking, prolonged hospital stays, and stress-related problems with milk flow. Fortunately, commercial formulas are good substitutes for breast milk, and bottle-feeding has some advantages. Bottles provide a way of measuring intake and provide fathers with the opportunity to share in the feeding routines. In addition, nipples can be modified or specialized nipples purchased for babies who have sucking difficulties or other problems coordinating their tongue, lips, and palate.

Whether they are being breast-fed or bottle-fed, preterm and developmentally delayed babies are likely to have problems with sucking. To suck, an infant must purse his lips around the nipple and rhythmically move his tongue up and down. This creates a vacuum that draws the milk into the infant's mouth, where it is reflexively swallowed. Problems can occur with babies who have difficulties with positioning, with pursing their lips, or with tongue control.

Whether the baby is being fed from breast or bottle, a beginning step to help a baby who is having difficulty with sucking is to modify the feeding environment.

- Make sure that the room is cool and quiet and that the lights are dim.

- Sit in a comfortable chair with an arm rest.

- Let the baby feel your skin or touch your breast as he sucks.

- Begin feeding, whenever possible, before your baby is crying frantically. A distraught baby may have difficulty sucking.

- If your baby tends to fall asleep after just a few sucks, awaken him fully before you begin the feeding. Keep a light on in the room and sing and talk to him during the feeding.

- If your baby is wide awake and crying before a feeding and then falls asleep as soon as he sucks on the nipple, it may be that your baby is seeking comfort rather than crying because he is hungry. Try to stretch out the feedings by giving him a pacifier when he awakens crying. If he rejects the pacifier at first, be persistent. If you hold the pacifier in his mouth as you rock and soothe him, he will gradually learn to accept it.

With a Breast-fed Baby

- Make sure that you are eating a well-balanced diet; avoid chocolate, spicy foods, caffeine, and over-the-counter medications.

- Drink plenty of water throughout the day.

- Try to get a few minutes' rest before you begin to breast-feed. When you are feeling relaxed, your baby's hunger cry will trigger a let-down reflex, and your milk will begin to flow spontaneously.

- Position your baby for breast-feeding by placing him in the crook of your arm with your hand supporting his buttocks.

- If your milk does not start dripping spontaneously, expel a few drops manually from your breast to get the feeding started.

- When you put your baby to the breast, rub your nipple on his cheek. This will stimulate him to turn his head, open his mouth, and actively search for the nipple.

- Aim the nipple toward your baby's mouth by holding your breast around the areola.

- Make sure that your baby gets the whole areola into his mouth and not just the nipple. Compressing or flattening the areola with your hand just before the baby begins sucking may be helpful.

- Make sure that the baby's nostrils are not covered by your breast.

- Never pull the nipple out of your baby's mouth. If your baby chews on the nipple, insert your finger in the side of his mouth and ease the nipple out gradually.

- Breast-feed on demand.

- Regardless of how much milk you feel your baby has taken in, limit each feeding to 15 to 20 minutes per side.

- Feed your baby with both breasts at every feeding.

- If your baby resists the breast, discontinue the feeding temporarily. Soothe your baby and try again.

- Try using a breast pump for a few days to increase the flow of milk.

If you are having trouble with your nipples, La Leche League has excellent pamphlets on nipple care, or consult your obstetrician. Do not get discouraged if it takes a week or two to establish a comfortable routine. If your baby continues to have difficulty with breast-feeding, call your pediatrician.

If you would like additional suggestions for breast-feeding your baby, there are several good books on the subject. *The Complete Book of Breastfeeding* by Lois Eichler and *Special Pamphlets for Special Babies* by Sarah Coulter Dunner and Edward Cerutti contain many useful ideas.

With a Bottle-fed Baby

- Experiment with positions until you find the most comfortable position for both you and the baby.

- Adjust the size of the nipple hole to accommodate to your baby. If he keeps choking, the nipple hole may be too large, and if he falls asleep without getting enough milk, it may be too small.

- Experiment with different types of nipples.

- Throw nipples away when they begin to get soft and gummy.

- Some babies enjoy soft music while they are feeding. Try it with your baby.

- Make sure to let your pediatrician know if problems with sucking persist.

Colic

Colic is a common digestive disorder that affects many young infants, whether or not they are premature or disabled. A baby who has colic experiences abdominal distress during or right after feeding. Often a baby will appear to be hungry and search frantically for the nipple. Then after a couple of sucks the baby will reject the nipple, draw up his legs, and cry out in pain. These attacks of colic may occur once or several times in the course of the day.

Although colic is disturbing to parents as well as infants, it is not a serious condition. It is simply an indication of an immature digestive system and is likely to disappear by the time the baby is three months old. While some "colicky" babies do better with a change of formula, for the most part colic is something that the baby simply must outgrow. Some pediatricians claim that colicky babies may be somewhat soothed by the sensation of riding in a car. There is even a device available now that attaches to a crib and simulates the sound and movement of a car. But for the most part, the best you can do is try to make your baby as comfortable as possible. Try carrying him on your shoulder, stretching him stomach down across your knee, swaying or moving up and down while you carry him, or rocking him in a cradle or car-bed.

Spoon-feeding

Problems feeding handicapped infants are not limited to finding the right nipple. Many handicapped babies have real difficulties managing baby food. A hypersensitive baby, or one who adjusts slowly to change, may have difficulty adjusting to the sensation of food in his mouth. A child with abnormal tone may either bite down too soon on the spoon and prevent the food from entering his mouth or not close his jaw at all. This happens frequently with cerebral palsy babies. The Down syndrome baby is likely to push the food out of his mouth with his tongue.

Babies who have difficulty accepting food into their mouths will also have problems chewing. They may not be able to achieve the rhythmic movement of the jaws or to use their tongues to move the food around.

To help your child accept food:

- Make sure that your baby is looking at you before you put the spoon in his mouth.

- Use a small, rounded spoon. Make sure the spoon is at room temperature before you put it in your baby's mouth.

- Feed your baby small amounts at a time and place the food well in the back of his mouth.

- Begin by giving your baby cereal for which you can control the consistency. Finding the exact consistency that is right for your baby is a matter of trial and error.

- If your baby is sensitive to temperature, make sure the food is at room temperature.

- Never introduce more than one new food at a time.

- Stop feeding your baby when he shows the first signs of disinterest. Never force your baby to eat.

Babies with developmental disabilities are often prone to hiccups. Hiccups are a spasm of the diaphragm and are usually of no consequence. Hiccups usually disappear within a few minutes, whether or not you give the baby a bottle. If hiccups persist for more than 12 hours, call your pediatrician.

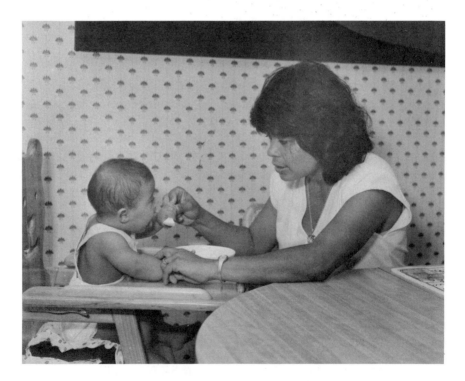

Many babies, handicapped or not, are likely to spit up small amounts of food after a feeding. Spitting up in immature babies is usually caused by esophageal reflux. The muscular part of the esophagus that normally keeps food from backing up functions improperly, and the food surges back from the stomach. If spitting up is excessive (a large amount at every feeding), call your pediatrician.

To limit hiccups and spitting up:

• Feed your baby frequently and on demand.

• Make sure to burp your baby several times during the feeding. Some babies burp more easily if held over your shoulder. Other babies do better if you lean them forward in a sitting position, holding up their chin with your hand. It may help to rub your baby's back gently, but do not slap or pound his back.

• Hold your baby in a sitting position for a few minutes after each feeding.

• If your baby is on formula you may want to try thickening the milk with a little rice cereal.

As long as your baby continues to gain weight and look healthy, don't worry about a little spitting up. In most situations the best solution with a young baby is to keep a diaper or towel handy to wipe up.

Dressing, Diapering, and Bathing

Simple routines like dressing, diapering, and bathing can become a challenge with babies who are hypersensitive or with babies who have poor postural control.

With hypersensitive babies there is always a fine line between overdressing and underdressing. Dressing the baby in an undershirt and an overshirt provides you with some flexibility if your baby tends to get too warm as the day goes on. Hypersensitive babies are also sensitive to changes in texture. A stiff outfit or a tag in the back of a shirt is enough to make some babies irritable. Be sure to wash all new baby things with a mild soap and double rinse to avoid irritation.

Babies with postural disorders or motor dysfunctions provide other challenges. A cerebral palsy baby may scissor her legs when you try to put on slacks or develop clonus (ankle spasms) or toe curling when you try to put on her shoes. If your baby is difficult to dress, it may help to modify her clothes. Babies can usually get along without shoes, and loose-fitting two-piece outfits can simplify the dressing chore.

Comforting

All babies at some time have uncontrollable crying spells when nothing the parent can do does any good. With developmentally disabled babies, these crying spells may occur more frequently, and parents can find them exhausting. This is particularly true with babies who have an abnormally high or piercing cry.

There are no universal guidelines for quieting a crying baby. Strategies that work for one baby may have a reverse effect on another, and strategies that work well one day may not work at all the next.

Here are some strategies that work with some babies at least some of the time:

- Offer your baby a bottle, breast, or pacifier. If she rejects it, take it away but try again a few seconds later. A very hungry baby may be too upset to recognize the nipple. If your baby refuses a pacifier when upset, you may want to reintroduce it when she is playful or calm. Once she has learned to suck a pacifier, she may be able to use it for self-calming.

- Wrap your baby in a light blanket so that her arms are close to her body and her thumb can reach her mouth.

- Hold your baby up to your shoulder and rock back and forth or from side to side.

- Place your baby across your knees on her belly and sway gently back and forth.

- Put your baby in a carrier or sling and walk around the house.

- Rock your baby in a stroller or move it back and forth.

- Place your baby in a crib, bassinette, or cradle, and pat her gently.

- Sing to your baby, put on the radio, or play a music box. Cuddly toys with tapes inside that mimic the swooshing sound in the uterus are comforting to some babies.

Putting Your Baby to Sleep

Sleep problems are common with developmentally disabled babies. They usually take longer to settle into a routine and may awaken frequently and for long stretches during the night. Another problem may be sleep position. A child who lacks neuromuscular control may not be able to readjust her posture during sleep. Still another problem may be parental concern. Parents of disabled babies may rush into the room before their baby has a chance to put herself back to sleep.

These suggestions may help your child form successful sleep habits:

- Put your baby to sleep in the same place and at approximately the same time every night. Sleeping is habit-forming!

- Let your baby fall asleep in her crib or cradle rather than in your arms. It is important for her to associate the crib with falling asleep.

- Find a soft blanket that your baby seems to like, and keep it in the crib at all times. The blanket can be an extra cue that will help your baby fall asleep.

- If your baby is six months old or more, avoid giving her a bottle right before she falls asleep. A very wet diaper is disturbing.

- Help your baby learn to sleep through the night. Rather than picking your baby up as soon as she begins to cry, give her a reassuring pat and let her fall back to sleep.

- If the pat didn't work and your baby begins to cry again, wait four or five minutes and pat her gently again.

- Unless you are willing to keep it up for a very long time, avoid the temptation of putting your baby in your bed.

If you would like to read more about sleep problems and solutions, *Crying Baby, Sleepless Nights* by Sandy Jones is an excellent reference.

Working Out a Daily Routine

In the first section of *In Time and With Love* we discussed the importance of leaving time for yourself. One of the best ways to accomplish this is to begin to schedule your baby. Advice about scheduling varies greatly. In the pre–Dr. Spock era, babies were scheduled by the minute hand. In the post-Spock era, demand feeding was the rule. We tend to disagree with both positions. Most babies do better on a schedule as long as it isn't rigid. Most important, all parents, no matter how dedicated they are to their baby, need time for themselves and time to be together.

As you begin to schedule your baby, pay attention to the cyclical patterns your baby has developed on his own. Does our baby have a particular time during the day when he is more likely to be fussy or playful? Give your baby a bath at the same time every day. If your baby is relaxed by a bath, choose the time of day when your baby is most likely to fuss. If weather permits, take your baby on an outing at the same time every day. If you like to sing, select a jaunty tune for playtime and a quiet song for sleep time. After a while, your baby will associate a tune with playing or falling asleep. Dim the lights when it is sleep time, and make them bright for playtime. Gradually stretch out the time between feedings by giving your baby water or a pacifier.

Arranging Your Baby's Environment

No matter how much planning you do, it is difficult to arrange the house to accommodate the baby until you have the baby home and find out what you need. And your needs will change as your baby grows older. But be sure to baby-proof your house before your baby starts to creep around.

Before putting up mobiles, pictures, and crib toys, think about your baby's temperament. If your baby is sensitive to loud noises, take his tolerance level into account as you choose musical toys. Make sure not to put up a sound mobile that you cannot turn off. If your baby is overly quiet and placid, you may want to encourage alertness with stimulating mobiles, chimes, and musical toys.

Arrange your house so that there is a comfortable place for your baby in each room where you spend a lot of time. This may involve buying or improvising an extra cradle or bassinette. If your baby spits up after feeding, you may want to put a plastic tablecloth under the feeding chair.

Post emergency telephone numbers beside every telephone. Hopefully, you will not have to use them.

Take into account your baby's particular type of disability as you arrange the house. Visually impaired babies need an environment in which there is tactile and auditory stimulation and cues. An area rug in the bedroom could define play space for your baby and keep him from bumping into furniture.

Hearing-impaired babies need special opportunities to develop residual hearing. Hanging a bell by your baby's door lets you signal to your baby that you are coming into the room.

Babies with mobility problems need the opportunity to see the world from different perspectives. Keep a stroller in the house so you can wheel your baby from room to room, or carry your baby in a "Snuggly," or other baby carrier. Arrange places in different rooms where your baby can be propped in a safe and comfortable sitting position.

When a baby has a disability, the routines of daily living are seldom routine. With some babies, some of the routines are especially easy. A preterm baby may fall asleep easily after feeding, and a baby who is slow in motor development may not pose a threat to house plants or bric-a-brac. More frequently, the daily care of a special needs baby puts heavy demands on the household. On one hand, these demands can push you to the point of exhaustion. On the other hand, the persistent demands of your baby strengthen the bond between parent and child.

8

Discipline
and Social Skills

Babies who have a tough beginning physically often exhibit difficult behavior when they reach the toddler stage. This is not surprising. The baby who had trouble organizing his behavior during infancy is likely to exhibit some disorganization as he faces the new demands of the toddler period. At the same time, as a parent of a special needs child you may not be in a hurry to impose limits on your toddler. You recognize that some misbehavior is a sign of developmental progress, so you are happy to see your toddler misbehaving.

All children, even when development is normal, have problems with developmental control during toddlerhood. They have to accept the fact that their needs will not be met immediately and that they can't always have their way. They also need to develop self-regulating techniques, ways of calming themselves down when they are upset or overly excited. For toddlers with special needs, these lessons are hard to learn.

Setting Limits

Parents of nonhandicapped children recognize the importance of providing behavioral guidelines and setting consistent limits. They recognize that allowing their child to have and do whatever he wants is irresponsible, and that their child must learn to live in harmony with other people. When we ask parents if the same principles hold for their disabled child, the answer is very often, "Yes, but . . ."

". . . but he really doesn't understand about not breaking his brother's toys."

". . . but we can't say 'no' to him. He gets into terrible tantrums and can't get himself out of them."

". . . but right now our concern is to get him healthy."

". . . but he has a right to scream and lash out. How would you like to be blind?"

As we listen to parents give reasons for not disciplining their handicapped children, we recognize their dilemma. Saying "no" and imposing limits are much more difficult with a handicapped child. Parents who continue to blame themselves for their child's problem feel guilty when they discipline. Parents with children who are physically fragile are fearful of endangering their child's health. Parents who have mixed feelings toward their handicapped child may feel paralyzed when it comes to discipline.

Despite the difficulties associated with discipline, a lack of behavioral limits can be devastating to a child. When parents give up the responsibility of helping their child develop socially appropriate behavior, they are imposing an extra handicap that their child may never outgrow.

- When children have learned to attend to differences in their parents' tone and expression, they are ready to learn the meaning of "no."

- In the beginning reserve the word "no" for situations with a clear-cut danger. Say "No, hot" as you pull your child away from the stove. Whenever possible, get your child to look at you when you are saying "no."

- Always keep your voice calm and firm when you say "no" and simultaneously remove the child from the danger or the danger from the child.

- Always provide your child with an alternative. He may not dig up the house plants, but he may dig in the sand.

- Remember that special needs children may take longer than other children to understand the meaning of "no." If your child stops for a minute, looks at you, and then continues with the prohibited behavior, it is a good sign. He is beginning to make the connection. Be persistent. After a while he will understand that "no" means "stop."

- If your child continues the prohibited behavior after three or four trials it is time to distract him. Learning "no" takes time.

Responsibilities

Children who are ready to learn the meaning of "no" are also ready to learn the meaning of "yes." As you teach your child to hand you the napkin,

throw away the banana peel, or pick up a toy, you are giving your child a first lesson in taking responsibility. At the same time you are helping her engage in behaviors that gain your approval and applause.

When your child has the ability to do a simple chore, seek out every opportunity to let her practice, and give her praise and encouragement. For example, if your child is ready to throw, give her a chance to throw a piece of paper in the wastebasket and thank her for being a big girl.

If your child half-completes a chore, praise her for what she has done rather than criticize her for what she has not done. For example, if your child gets distracted in the middle of picking up her toys, you might say, "I like the way you picked up all your blocks. Do you suppose you could pick up your stuffed animals? They don't like it on the floor."

Sing some simple songs with her that go along with her chores. "It's clean-up time, it's clean-up time. Everybody helps with clean up-time." Or, "This is the way we pick up the blocks, pick up the blocks, pick up the blocks. This is the way we pick up the blocks, so early in the morning."

Temper Tantrums

Temper tantrums are a part of the behavioral repertoire of practically every toddler. Unfortunately, with special needs children, temper tantrums may be more frequent, longer lasting, and harder to prevent or control.

If your child throws a temper tantrum, observe the following rules:

- Do not shout or try to impose discipline while the tantrum is going on.

- Never hit, spank, or shake your baby. Shaking is particularly dangerous for infants because it can cause brain damage.

- Put your child in a safe place and remain aloof and nonjudgmental until the tantrum is over.

- If your child's behavior is out of control, so that she doesn't know what she is upset about, you may have to help her calm down. Pat her gently. Hold and rock her, but don't take back the "no" that got the tantrum started.

Aggressive Behavior

Never let your child physically hurt you or another person. Although you may think it's cute when an 18-month-old baby gets cross and gives you a slap, if hitting gets to be a habit it isn't cute anymore. Furthermore, it is very difficult for a child to learn that it is okay to hit Mommy or Daddy but it is not okay to hit a baby or a dog. *The no hitting, no biting, no hurting rule must have no exceptions.*

Here are some ways you can help your child learn this rule:

- If your child hits you or anyone else, your immediate response should be, "No hitting."

- Help your child learn the difference between hitting and stroking. If she hits the dog, say, "No hitting, make nice." Be sure to praise her when she strokes the dog.

- If your child hits another child, take her away from the child immediately and repeat the admonition, "No hitting."

- If your child persists in hitting or biting, begin a time-out procedure. Tell the child what she did wrong and what is going to happen. "No hitting. You have to sit in the time-out chair." Sit your child in a chair away from the play for a brief period. (It sometimes helps to use an egg-timer.) Until your child understands the time-out procedure, you may have to hold her in the chair. Face your child in the chair away from you and hold her gently but firmly. If your child plays nicely after a time-out period, be quick to praise her: "I like the way you're playing."

Controlling Harmful Behavior

Parents of special needs children are disturbed when their toddlers engage in harmful behavior. With some behaviors, such as head-banging, the concern is that the child is going to hurt himself. With other behaviors, such as spinning or hand-waving, they are concerned about the baby's appearance. Parents are right to pay attention to "self-stimulating" behaviors. Once the behaviors begin they can easily become a habit.

Some babies head-bang when they are having a temper tantrum. Other babies head-bang because they find it pleasurable. The best way to prevent head-banging is to cushion your baby's head. Depending on where he is banging his head, pad the back and the side of the crib, use a waterbed mattress, or put a cushioned helmet on your baby's head. Without the bang, head-banging loses its appeal.

If your baby is in the habit of spinning or hand-waving, keep him busy and interested in toys and games.

If your toddler has lost interest in playing with his toys, place him in a swing or hammock or on a rocking horse. This will provide the motion he is looking for without becoming habit forming.

Developing Social Skills

Although we are likely to think of behavioral management as controlling bad behaviors, a more important component of behavioral management is teaching social skills. Special needs children are likely to spend a great deal of time around adults where they don't have to share toys, take turns, or even make social overtures. Parents of special needs children need to work hard at finding peers for their children to play with.

Many special needs children shy away from other children. A child who is temperamentally shy, slow to warm up, or easily overstimulated may not be comfortable around other children. If your child withdraws or becomes

irritable when he is with other children, introduce him to one child at a time. Select a child who is either much older or much younger, so that your child will not feel threatened by a peer.

Praise your child for all friendly overtures even if your child does no more than watch other children who are playing.

Do not expect your child to share toys spontaneously. Your child has just learned the meaning of "mine," and it is difficult to make the distinction between sharing a toy and giving a toy away. It is easier to teach children turn-taking with toys than to introduce the idea of sharing.

When children with special needs are ready to begin a school situation, the most important challenges they will face are controlling impulsive behavior and getting along with other children. If you begin as early as possible to help your child accept limits, take responsibility, control aggressive behavior, and play with other children, he will have a much better chance of doing well in school. With many children the problem in school is not that they cannot learn but that they have learned maladaptive behaviors that interfere with learning.

PART III

PLAYING
and
LEARNING

"I'm so confused. Every time I bring my baby to a different specialist, I get told something different. One tells me stimulate, the other tells me take it easy. One says take her out, the next one says keep her home. One says physical therapy now, the next one says wait."

Time and again parents describe the frustration of conflicting advice. Therapists do not always agree on the timing or the value of therapy. Professionals who have seen parents exhaust themselves and their baby with an overdose of therapeutic intervention might advise parents to go easy. Others, who have seen babies flourish on a therapeutic program, may be more likely to suggest intervention. All professionals do agree, however, that whether or not a structured therapeutic program is initiated, all babies benefit from developmentally appropriate play with their parents.

In Part III we help you identify the developmental stage or stages your baby is experiencing. We suggest stage-appropriate activities that you and your baby will enjoy, regardless of your baby's chronological age.

Taking into account the broad range of individual differences, we attempt to identify emerging behaviors and subtle accomplishments that signal developmental progress. Many of the behaviors we describe emerge spontaneously, and we suggest that you take on the role of observer. At other times the introduction of a toy or the retelling of a simple story may be an appropriate way to support an emerging skill.

Chapter 9 focuses on social and emotional development. We describe ways of enhancing the love relationship between parent and baby and promoting self-awareness. In Chapter 10, we investigate the development of balance and other motor skills and suggest games and activities that encourage their development. In Chapter 11 the emphasis is on language. We look at the infant's growing capacity to learn the meaning of spoken language and describe the role of the parent as the baby's language teacher. In Chapter 12, we examine the development of problem-solving skills. We describe how babies reach out and experiment with solving problems, adapting to change, facing new challenges, and making new discoveries.

The rate and course of development are difficult to predict in any baby, disabled or not. With some children the development of social, motor, language and cognitive skills proceeds at the same pace. For other babies one system serves as the developmental forerunner. Still other babies change in surprising ways, with different systems taking the lead at different times.

A second important way babies differ from each other is in their developmental timetable. Some babies seem to be in a hurry about development, and parents have to stay on their toes to keep up with the stages. For other babies, development proceeds at a more leisurely pace. Frequently periods of growth are followed by periods of consolidation, where development seems to be at a standstill. Occasionally a baby follows an idiosyncratic pattern, learning supposedly harder tasks before acquiring skills that are considered easier for most babies.

Part III describes the developmental events that take place in the early months and years and suggests how parents can encourage emerging skills and provide productive input. The goal is not to rush the developmental process, but to help you tune in to your baby's unique needs and responses. We believe the activities you select are exactly right when your baby is making progress and you and your baby are having fun together.

9

Promoting
Self-Awareness

"When the doctor told me my baby had spina bifida, I didn't want to see her. I wanted them to take her away and put her in an institution. I knew that if they ever put her in my arms she would be mine and I would love her."

Babies come into the world uniquely programmed to win their parents' love. With few exceptions, a newborn baby has the built-in capacity to focus on his mother's face and to tune into his mother's voice. The mother, too, is programmed to respond. The softness of the baby's skin invites the mother's stroke, and milk flows in the nursing mother in response to the baby's cry.

In this chapter and subsequent chapters in this section, we trace infant development through three qualitatively different stages. In the first stage, Tuning In, babies are adjusting to life outside the uterus. Equipped with a built-in capacity to recognize likes and differences, babies listen to voices, make eye contact, and experience the comfort of touch. In the second stage, Reaching Out, babies actively initiate contact with the world of objects and people and anticipate a response. In the third stage, Making Discoveries, babies explore objects and social relationships and are actively involved in goal-oriented behaviors. Babies enter these stages at different chronological ages, and often the stages overlap.

Tuning In

In the first stage, parent and infant develop a special kind of closeness that is rooted in biology. Psychologists call this close relationship *bonding*, and describe it as a love affair between parent and child. The baby, who has lost the safety and predictability of life inside the uterus, is protected outside the uterus by the strength of parental love.

When babies are born full term with a well-organized nervous system, a mutually supportive relationship between baby and mother begins at birth. Nursing releases a hormone into the mother's system that gives her a feeling of well-being as she nourishes her baby. The baby responds to the gentle stroking, rocking, and soothing of his mother by becoming quiet, alert, and organized. Preterm or "at risk" babies are not as well-organized as healthy full-term babies. They may be easily overwhelmed by new sensations and may have difficulty regaining their composure. With babies who are disorganized and difficult to soothe, a mutually supportive relationship between parent and infant may take longer to achieve.

As parents and infants play out their love affair during the Tuning In stage, several important developments are taking place simultaneously. Babies are spending a greater amount of time in the quiet alert state, allowing them to focus on their environment. They are becoming increasingly aware of the potential of their own bodies. They are learning ways to comfort themselves when the stress in their environment is more than they can handle, and they are learning the joy of social interactions.

Help your baby maintain a state of quiet alertness. The longer your baby remains quiet and alert, the more opportunities he will have to take in new information.

- Speak to your baby gently as he is awakening, before he starts to cry. Try to maintain eye contact.

- When your baby is crying, lift him onto your shoulder and let him focus on a face or interesting object.

Help your baby learn about his body. As your baby kicks his feet, gazes at his hands, or strokes your face with his fingers, he is making important discoveries about his own body and its many capabilities.

- Give your baby the opportunity to watch the movement of his own hands. Babies get very excited when they first discover

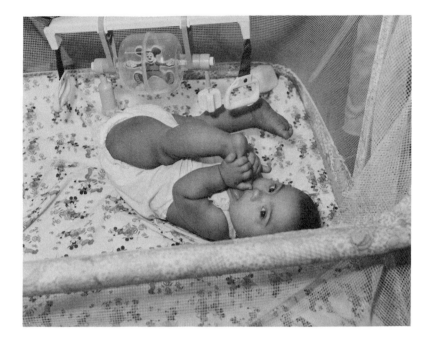

what fun it is to wave their fingers in front of their eyes. When your baby lets his fingers fall out of sight, he may appear upset. It takes a baby a while to coordinate his hands and eyes and to realize that he has the power to put his hand back into his visual field.

- Place a colorful sock on one of your baby's hands. It will increase the fun of hand-watching and help your baby with the ongoing task of learning about himself.

- Bath time provides an excellent opportunity to increase body awareness. Massage your baby's arms and fingers, then legs and toes, as you dry him after his bath.

- When the temperature of the room is appropriate, give your baby an opportunity to kick his legs without wearing a diaper. This self-generated activity helps him learn how his body is organized.

Babies differ from each other in the kinds of stimulation they find stressful, in the amount of stress they can tolerate without becoming disrupted, and in the strategies they develop to cope with stress. While you should be concerned with protecting your baby from overly stressful situations, you also ought to give your baby opportunities to develop coping strategies. By watching your baby closely and experimenting with different techniques, you will find ways to help your child deal with stress.

- Some babies quiet down when you place your hand gently on their backs or stomachs. Other babies quiet when you talk to them in a low, steady voice.

- Help your baby find ways to self-comfort. Position him in the crib with his thumb close to his mouth to encourage sucking.

- Teach your baby to use a pacifier as a means of self-comforting. Be sure to introduce your baby to the pacifier when he is in a relaxed and happy mood. If you wait until he is upset, he is very likely to reject it.

Help your baby take part in social interactions. Your baby has a natural capacity to socialize. From the moment of birth a baby is most attentive and alert when he can see his mother's face and listen to her voice. As mothers and fathers engage their babies in back-and-forth conversations and playful interactions, they foster the development of their baby's social skills.

- Carry on conversations with your baby at every opportunity, especially when you are holding him. Sing, hum, or talk softly with exaggerated changes in pitch and wait for him to answer. You will always be his best and favorite toy.

- Lie flat on your back and hold your baby in the air. He will be interested in seeing your face from a different perspective.

- When you are holding your baby, let him touch your face and feel your skin. Your baby is coming to know you as mother or father by the sound of your voice, the way you hold him, the way you look, and the way you feel.

- Provide opportunities for the baby's father to carry on his own conversations. Fathers and mothers have different ways of playing, different voice qualities, and different textures, and it is important for your baby to have this double experience.

Be sensitive to your baby's cues. An animated conversation can be tiring. When your baby stops trying to coo or talk he is saying, "I've had enough for now." Babies who are small and not very strong may signal "I've had enough" in very subtle ways. They may grimace or yawn or shut their eyes. They may turn pale or red, start to shake, extend their arms, or perhaps turn limp. Be sensitive to your baby's way of telling you when he needs time out from stimulation.

Stage I Adaptations

For babies who are visually limited

*   Hang wind chimes in one or two rooms of the house in front of a window. When your baby is crying, lift him to your shoulder and let him hear the tinkling of the chimes.

*   Help your baby discover his own hands by placing bands with bells on your baby's wrists. As he moves his hands in front of him he will hear the ringing of the bells. (You can make a wristband by cutting off the cuff of an infant sock, sewing the bell securely on the inside, folding the cuff over the bell, and sewing the seam shut.)

*   Wear a special cologne to help your baby recognize you as you approach the crib.

For babies who are hearing impaired

*   When your baby is in a state of quiet alertness, place your lips close to his ear and talk softly. Give each ear a turn. Speaking directly into your baby's ear is like fitting him with a hearing aid.

*   Wear a special cologne that your baby will recognize. This will help him know you are coming when he cannot hear your voice.

For babies who are physically impaired

*   If your baby has difficulty with arm control, position him in

your lap with his arms in front of him. Place his hands together so that he has the sensation of feeling his own hands.

- Hold your baby's hand and help him stroke your face and feel your nose and mouth. Blow gently when his fingers are over your mouth.

For babies who are hypersensitive or tactile defensive

If your baby is hypersensitive to touch (tactile defensive) and gets upset or withdrawn when you hold or stroke him, you will have to help him adapt to new sensations.

- If he is tactile defensive and flaccid or floppy, stroke his arms and legs with a firm and steady stroke. If he tends to be rigid and jittery, use a more gentle touch and avoid sudden movements.

- Some tactile defensive babies will tolerate and even enjoy gentle stroking with a feather or a paintbrush.

- Tactile defensive babies are likely to reject a pacifier. Try different kinds of pacifiers until you find one your baby will accept. A Sassy pacifier is especially good for small babies with a weak sucking reflex.

For babies with Down syndrome

Babies with Down syndrome may take longer to respond to stimulation and may be more muted in their responses than other babies.

- Be patient with your baby. It may take him a month or more before he can sustain a state of quiet alertness.

- When your baby establishes eye contact with you, do not expect an immediate smile or cooing. Your baby will learn to smile and coo, but it may take longer than you expect.

- Continue to talk to your baby even when you do not get a distinct response. Your baby is aware of your overtures and will learn to respond in time.

Reaching Out

The second stage of development, Reaching Out, is characterized by your baby's growing ability to initiate social interactions. Your baby is becoming more and more social, reaching out her arms to an approaching parent, actively seeking out people to engage in vocal play. In the early phase of Reaching Out your baby smiles happily at anyone who smiles back. After a while she becomes more discriminatory, reserving her biggest greetings for the people who are most familiar.

In the first developmental stage, self-awareness was characterized by your baby's ability to recognize and coordinate different parts of her body. Now your baby is exploring the relationship between her own body and the outside world. She is reaching out for the mobile over her crib, smiling at herself in the mirror, picking up a cracker and putting it in her mouth. At the same time she is making new discoveries about her own body, discovering a set of toes, passing toys from hand to hand, and pulling at one ear and then the other.

A few props can help increase your baby's self-awareness:

- Put up a safety mirror over the changing table or inside the crib. Your baby will enjoy getting acquainted with her own image.

- Put colorful socks on your baby's feet. Now that she has discovered where to find her toes, you can add an element of surprise.

- Give your baby some special practice bringing her hand to her mouth. Let her dip her finger in her cereal or fruit, even if she gets a bit messy.

Increase opportunities for social interaction. Your baby's social world is expanding. She not only makes distinctions between mother and father, she is making distinctions between children and adults and between old friends and strangers. She is fascinated with other children and delighted by a playful sibling.

As your baby develops an increased capacity to remember past experiences, you will see a change in reactions to new people. She will become wary when a stranger gets too close. You will also notice a difference in the way your baby relates to you. Your baby will become watchful when you start to leave the room and give you a special greeting when you return. This special love for special people is called *attachment behavior*. It begins in the second developmental stage and continues through the third stage.

Just as special needs babies may differ in their development timetable from other babies, they may differ in their attachment behavior. Some special needs babies take longer to develop attachment and continue to interact with anyone who is willing to play. Other special needs babies appear to get overattached and have difficulty with any kind of separation.

Playing games with your baby that involve separating and coming back together helps to strengthen attachment behavior and give your baby the assurance that you will always reappear:

- Play different versions of the peek-a-boo game. Peek-a-boo allows your baby to know that you can be out of sight for a second without disappearing. Put your hands over your face, and take them away quickly, saying, "Peek-a-boo!" Put a scarf over your baby's head and pull it off quickly, saying, "Peek-a-boo!"

- Parachute is a more elaborate form of peek-a-boo that is fun when there are several adults. A sheet is a good substitute for a parachute.

- Interactive pull-push games help your baby understand that mother or father can go away and come back. If your baby is strong enough to sit with support, see-saw is a good push-pull game. Sit face to face with your baby and hold her hands. As you recite "See-saw, Margery Daw," lean backwards and come forwards. Then help your baby take a turn leaning backwards and forwards.

- Play catch with your baby. Sit her in a corner. Push a beach ball toward her and let her push it back. During this game—as with any game—talk about what you are doing. When you push the brightly colored beach ball to your baby, say, "Here comes the ball! Whee, you caught it! Good, now push it to Daddy."

- Hold one end of a scarf and let your baby hold onto the other end. Pull tight and then let loose. See if your baby will join the game.

With an increased capacity to hold an image in memory, your baby is ready for interactive games involving imitation and anticipation.

- Show your baby a Jack-in-the-box. Does she laugh out loud when Jack pops out of the box?

- Turn a cake pan over and bang on it. See if your baby will imitate the banging.

- Blow bubbles for your baby. She will enjoy watching them float away. She might even imitate your blowing.

- Sing the song "Trot, Trot to Boston" or "Pop Goes the Weasel." See if your baby laughs as you come to the last stanza. In "Trot, Trot to Boston" let your baby drop half-way through your knees at the end. In "Pop Goes the Weasel," turn in a circle and lift her in the air when you come to "Pop."

Stage 2 Adaptations

For babies who are visually limited

- Guide your baby through a tasting experience. Place her hand in the cereal and then in her mouth. After a while she will finger feed herself.

- Place socks with bells on your baby's feet. Make sure that the bells are *very securely* sewn on.

- Use very bright multicolored beach balls for your rolling-back-and-forth games.

For babies who are hearing impaired

• Before you initiate a back-and-forth game with your baby, be sure to establish eye contact. Let your baby feel your lips as you begin to talk.

• When you sing a song to your baby, bounce your baby on your knee in rhythm with the song. Your baby will feel the rhythm of your speech.

• Continue to talk to your baby even though she may not babble back.

• Hold your baby's hand in front of your mouth as you chant these rhymes:

> *Ba, Ba, Ba, Bumblebee*
> *Ba, Ba, Ba, Bumblebee*
> *I will say Ba to you*
> *You will say Ba to me.*

> *Pop, pop, pop, pop*
> *My popcorn pops*
> *Pop, pop, pop, pop*
> *And now it stops.*

For babies who are physically impaired

• Play a special version of the pull-push game. Place your baby on a mat between you and your spouse. Take turns pulling baby and mat toward you. Greet the baby with a special "Hi" as you pull her to your side.

• Invent your own modification of "Trot, Trot to Boston" and "Pop Goes the Weasel." If your baby cannot sit up, you can move her legs up and down as you recite "Pop Goes the Weasel." When you reach the "Pop," release your baby's legs for a second and then catch them again.

• Avoid quick movements in all the games you play so that your baby will not be startled.

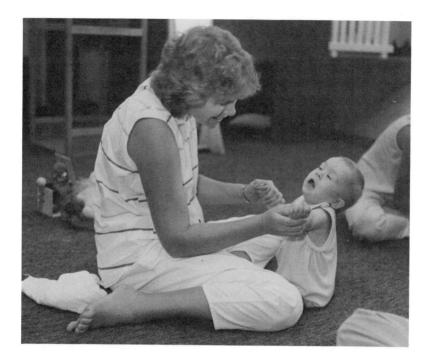

For babies who are hypersensitive or tactile defensive

- Play a special version of see-saw. Thread a long silk scarf through a paper towel spindle and tie the ends together. Place the scarf around your baby's back when she is in a half-sitting position. Put your baby's hands and yours on the spindle. See-saw gently up and down.

- Use a crib sheet as a hammock. Let your partner hold one end while you hold the other. Gently swing your baby in the hammock as you sing "Rock-a-bye Baby." When you come to "the cradle will fall," drop the hammock gently and give your baby a kiss.

- Your baby may not like sticky fingers. When you play the finger food game, use water instead of cereal.

For babies with Down syndrome

Select games and activities that you and your baby enjoy. If your baby does not show a visible reaction to a game such as bubble blowing or cake pan, continue your efforts but do not play more vigorously. Remember that your baby may need some time to take in new information and express her delight. If you are playing the cake-pan-banging game, for instance, don't bang harder because she seems to ignore the first few bangs. A loud bang could turn off an emerging smile.

With all the games, keep in mind that you are not looking for perfect performance, but rather the fun of participation. Make sure you praise your baby for every beginning attempt.

Making Discoveries

In the third stage, Making Discoveries, your baby is interested not only in reaching out and exploring the world outside himself, but also in making discoveries about how things outside him are connected. He is exploring objects to see if they come apart or fit inside each other. He is exploring spaces and places: Can he fit himself inside a box or under the sofa? He is exploring relationships with other people: Can he make his mother laugh at his newest stunt?

As your baby practices his motor skills and plays rough-and-tumble games, he increases his knowledge of his own body and the ways the parts of his body are connected with each other. You can spot signs of developing self-awareness. When you play "This Little Piggy Went to Market" your baby will look down at his toes as soon as the game begins. If he gets a mosquito bite on his arm he will find the spot and scratch it.

Another indicator of increased self-awareness is a new level of mirror play. At some time during this stage your baby will make the connection between the baby in the mirror and himself. If you put a hat on his head and show him his image in the mirror, he will learn to reach for the hat. If you place a toy beside him while he is looking in the mirror, he will reach down and pick up the toy.

Perhaps the most exciting indicator of this new level of self-awareness is your baby's readiness to repeat a stunt that draws laughs. If he puts the salad bowl on his head and the family bursts out laughing, he will try it again. Your baby is telling you without words that he knows that he is a person and can make other people react to the things he does.

To help your baby make discoveries, try these games:

• While your baby is standing in front of the mirror put a toy beside him. Does he reach for the toy in the mirror, or does he look down at the floor?

• Put a piece of Scotch tape on your baby's toe and let him pull it off.

• Put a sticker in the middle of your baby's forehead and let him look at himself in a mirror. Does he watch his image in the mirror as he pulls the sticker off his forehead?

During Stage Three, your baby will demonstrate an increased awareness of others. He has become a people-watcher, interested and alert each time a new person comes into the house. He listens to adult conversations, watches facial expressions, and gives his own reactions in easy-to-read ways. If a new person approaches too quickly, he may bury his head in Daddy's shirt. If his sister or brother comes into the room, he can express his delight with happy squeals.

Help your baby explore his new-found awareness to others:

- Invite other children over to play. Remember that even when your child is ready to play around other children, you will need to be on hand. Babies don't understand sharing and can get into a struggle over toys. Take on the task of passing toys to your child and his friend—to keep the time a happy one.

- When a new person approaches your baby, discourage him or her from immediately lifting up the baby. Babies make friends more easily if the visitor gives them warming-up time and offers them a toy.

- Make separation easier for your child. Play a leave-taking game with your baby. Wave "Good-bye," leave the room for a second, and come back saying, "Hello."

As your baby becomes physically more adept, you will increasingly notice signs of psychological attachment. Your baby will keep a close watch on your whereabouts when a stranger is around or when you take him on a visit. He may be happy to explore new areas, but only if he can maintain eye contact with you and check back from time to time. When he comes on something new, he will look at you to make sure it is safe before he continues exploring. If you don't look frightened or horrified, he will continue to play.

Help your baby explore the relationship between together and apart with a few simple games:

- Play a game of tag with your baby using a hoop as the playing field.

- When your baby is good at crawling or creeping, play a simplified version of hide-and-seek.

- Play "I'm going to get you" games with your child.

One problem such young explorers face is distinguishing between rules of play and rules of day-to-day living. When parents say "no" in a firm voice, the baby will often stop what he is doing, look up for a second, and then proceed with the mischief. The baby is not making a distinction between a "no" that is for real and a "no" that is a back-and-forth game. It's hard for a baby to understand why splashing in the bathtub is encouraged and splashing in the toilet is forbidden, or why it's good to dig in the sandbox and bad to dig in the plant box.

Help your child explore with ease by making the distinction clear. Use a word like "dirty" or "yucky" when he gets into something you don't want him to touch. This changes the message from "I don't want you to explore" to "I don't want you touching that yucky thing."

In the Reaching Out stage your baby was able to imitate the actions that were in his repertoire. In the Discovery stage your baby's imitative skills are more advanced. With a better understanding of his body parts and how they work together, he is able to imitate actions that he hasn't tried before. If you pat your head or pull your ear, your baby may follow suit.

A second kind of imitation that is beginning to emerge is called "deferred imitation." Your baby will imitate an action several hours after he has seen it performed. If your baby has seen you talk on the telephone, he will pick

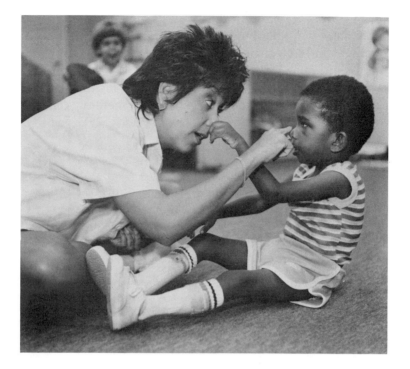

up the receiver and hold it to his ear. If your baby has seen you pat the dog, he will try out his own version of patting when the dog ventures into his territory.

Encourage your child to develop his imitating skills:

•   Play body-part games with your baby—"Touch your nose," "Touch your eyes," "Touch your mouth." After a while your baby will enjoy a more complicated version: he touches your nose and you touch his. When he can play touching games with some degree of success, you can create your own little songs to accompany the command.

>   *Touch my eye*
>   *Touch yours too.*
>   *First touch me*
>   *And then touch you.*

•   Play a copy-cat game like "So Big" or "Patty-Cake."

- Sing action songs with your baby, changing the words to match your baby's skills. "The Wheels on the Bus Go Round and Round" could become "The Wheels on the Bus Go Clang, Clang, Clang" as you and your baby clap knees.

Pretending is a sophisticated skill that is just beginning to emerge in the Discovery stage. Early pretending is an outgrowth of imitation. As with deferred imitation, your baby has to remember an action and replay his version of it later. When your child first starts to pretend, you will have difficulty making a distinction between pretend play and imitation. He picks up an empty cup and holds it to his mouth. Is he imitating you drinking coffee, or is he pretending to drink some milk? The distinction will become clearer as your baby continues to play. Perhaps he will offer his teddy bear a drink from the cup, or perhaps he will pick up an alphabet block and use it as a cup.

Make pretending fun and easy by providing the right props:

- Place old hats, shoes, and scarves in front of a mirror and watch what your baby does. Dress-up is a wonderful game to feed your baby's growing imagination.

- Give your baby some nonbreakable dishes and bring in stuffed animal "guests" to a tea party.

- Bring your baby a teddy bear and a blanket. Perhaps he'll put teddy to sleep.

- Give your baby a purse to play with. He may decide to go shopping.

Stage 3 Adaptations

For babies who are visually limited

- Play a special version of the mirror game. Place a band with a bell around his ankle. (Remember to sew the bell *securely* onto the band.) See if your baby reaches for his ankle and starts to finger the bell.

- Talk to your baby from the minute you enter the room. Do not stop talking until you have left the room.

- Hide-and-seek is a good game once your baby is mobile. First, make sure that there is nothing in the room that could hurt your baby, such as a table with sharp corners or a lamp cord. Move across the room and challenge your baby until he discovers where you are.

- If your baby is walking, play follow-the-leader by each holding on to a hula hoop. Talk to your baby about where you are walking. "We are walking on the sidewalk." "We are walking through the grass."

For babies who are hearing impaired

- Always begin a game by calling his name and getting his attention. You may want to say, "Thomas, it's playtime." If your child does not respond to your voice alone, hold his hand as you call his name.

- Use words when you play imitation games even if you think your child does not hear the words. Your child may have more residual hearing than you realize.

- Make sure that you play your games in a quiet room. Your baby will have trouble tuning in if there are competing sounds.

For babies who are physically impaired

- Provide "self-awareness" challenges that he can be successful with. For example, instead of putting Scotch tape on his toe, put a cotton pad between his toes.

- When you choose imitation games, make sure that your baby is able to perform the actions he is expected to copy. If your baby has difficulty with hand clapping, clap your hand on your knee and let your baby follow suit.

For babies who are hypersensitive or tactile defensive

- Your baby may not enjoy playing imitation games that include touching his face. Play the same game with a doll or large stuffed animal.

• Avoid playing imitation or pretend games that involve wearing a hat. Your baby may get so upset by the feel of a hat on his head that he doesn't want to play at all.

For babies with Down syndrome

Some babies with Down syndrome seem to have more fun playing with toys than with people. It may be that adults are not always as patient as toys and do not let the baby set the pace. When you play with your baby, don't be in a hurry. It takes time for your baby to join in the fun.

As you select activities from this chapter, don't be surprised if you find yourself choosing some games suggested for one stage and some games suggested for another. When we talk about activities that babies enjoy at a particular stage, we are making generalizations. But your baby has distinct needs and tastes. Select the games that you and your baby enjoy wherever you happen to find them. When you are both relaxed and having fun, you know that you have made good choices.

10

Developing
Motor Skills

"As far as John and I are concerned it was the best day in our lives. Andrew had been a real pain all day—constantly whining and fussing and refusing to take a nap. By the time we got him settled for the night we were both worn out. He hadn't been quiet for more than five minutes when he started calling again. I went into his room really mad. I couldn't believe my eyes. He had pulled himself up and he was standing in his crib. I shouted for John and the two of us just stood there and cried."

The development of gross motor skills and the achievement of motor milestones has a profound effect on all areas of a baby's development. The baby with poor head control may be slow to locate sounds or objects even if she has no visual or auditory problems. The baby who has difficulty with sitting may be slower than others in exploring the properties of objects because he has had less opportunity for two-handed manipulation.

This chapter describes motor development throughout the three developmental stages: Tuning In, Reaching Out, and Making Discoveries. Within each development stage we detail the motor skills the baby is working on and suggest ways parents can arrange the environment to enhance their development; we do not describe therapeutic intervention. If your baby has a motor problem and is being followed by a physical therapist, you may want to skip this chapter, or discuss the ideas with your therapist.

When discussing the development of motor skills in babies, many parents focus their attention on specific milestones such as sitting up, standing, or taking a first step. These events are genuine cause for celebration. While the importance of such milestones should not be minimized, we also need to recognize that the quality of the performance is just as important as the timing. Flipping accidentally from back to stomach is very different from a purposeful roll.

Whatever motor skills your baby is working on, you need to be aware of the subtle changes that are taking place in the quality of the movement. Is your baby pulling up with less effort? Does it take her less time to stand up? Does she pull up over and over again for the sheer joy of practicing? You also need to realize that the sequence as well as the rate of motor skill achievement differs for each baby. Some babies, even if they do not have disabilities, will skip one or more of the typical milestones. It is not true that all babies must crawl before creeping and creep before walking.

Tuning In

In the Tuning In stage of development, your baby is working on primary coordinations. She is learning to raise and turn her head as she watches a mobile, kick her legs rhythmically, and wiggle her fingers in front of her eyes. Each new skill she achieves gives her access to information that helps her understand her world.

Head Control

Head control is the first and certainly the most important motor skill your baby will develop. Head control is a component of all the motor milestones. Also, when your baby has good head control it will be easier for

her to track objects and identify the source of sounds. You can encourage
the development of head control in a variety of ways:

- Place your baby face down on the floor. Sit a doll or teddy
  bear in front of her. See if she will lift her head to look at the
  doll's face.

- Lie flat on the floor. Place the baby face down on your stomach. This position will encourage your baby to lift her head in
  order to watch your face.

- Hold your baby on your shoulder. Encourage her to look at a
  toy or out the window.

- Place your baby on a blanket on her stomach and pull the
  blanket slowly across the floor. She will improve both head
  control and balance as she enjoys this magic-carpet ride.

- When your baby has gained enough head control to hold up
  her head easily, you may want to hold her on a large beach
  ball. As you rock baby and ball back and forth very gently,
  your baby will hold up her head, strengthening the muscles in
  her neck.

• When head control is established, play see-saw with your baby, pulling her up to a sitting position. She will have the fun of seeing you from different positions while she is practicing head control.

Kicking

Babies have a natural inclination to kick when placed on their backs. At first they kick in an uneven and spasmodic way, but after a while their kicking becomes more rhythmic, and they appear to be peddling an invisible bicycle.

Kicking does more than give babies an opportunity to exercise. It is an important way for the baby to learn about her own body and how it is located in space. You can encourage your baby to try kicking by providing stimulating environments:

• When the room is warm place your baby on the floor on her back with just a diaper on. When she begins to kick, turn on some music. Does the tempo of the music affect the rate of her kicking?

• Play bicycle with your baby by moving her legs in a bicycle motion while she is on her back. Make sure to bicycle in a forward direction as an early preparation for walking.

• Place a large beach towel in the bottom of the bathtub and fill the tub with about two inches of water. While you are watching, let your baby lie on her back in the water and practice her kicking. She will enjoy the sound and feel of the splashing.

• Make a "kick-mobile" by tying rattles or bells onto short lengths of ribbon or elastic. String the mobile between two chairs. Place your baby on a mat on the floor between two chairs so that she can activate the "kick-mobile" and listen to the jingle of the bells. Safety check: Always stay close by when your baby has access to ribbon or elastic. There is always the chance of her getting entangled.

Hand and Arm Exercises

Most newborns hold their hands in a tight-fisted position and keep their arms close to their bodies. During the Tuning In stage your baby will learn to thrust her arms in play and open and close her fists. These new skills help keep the outside world within reach. Help guide your baby to use her hands and arms:

- Place your finger in your baby's palm. At first she will grasp it reflexively. After a while she will learn how to tighten and loosen her fingers.

- While your baby is on her back, move her arms gently up and down and in and out. Adding a rhyme to the exercise can turn it into a game.

  > *Up and down, up and down,*
  > *This is what we do.*
  > *Up and down, up and down,*
  > *This is fun for you.*

- Hold your baby between your legs in the bathtub and help her splash with her arms.

- Sing a familiar song with your baby as you clap her hands gently together. You might try "If you're happy and you know it, clap your hands!"

Stage I Adaptations

For babies who are visually limited

While sighted babies lift their heads for the joy of looking around them, babies who are visually limited do not have such impetus for gaining head control.

- A good way to help a very young visually limited baby strengthen her neck muscles and develop head control is to hold her against your shoulder in an upright position. Support her head with your hand just enough to keep her head from swaying or falling back.

- Bath play, where the fun is in the feel and the sound of the water, is particularly appropriate for the visually impaired baby.

- When you make a kick-mobile for your baby, make sure the sound effects are interesting. Use very pliable squeak toys, bells, and rattles.

For babies who are hearing impaired

Hearing-impaired babies need extra practice in head-lifting in order to build their neck muscles and gain good head control. Hearing babies hear a parent coming and naturally lift their heads to watch Mom or Dad approach.

- Call your baby by name in a loud, clear voice every time you approach the crib.

- Hold your baby over your shoulder as you introduce her to new sights around the house.

- Create a special kick-mobile or cradle gym that is appealing to your hearing-impaired baby. Substitute an interesting sight for an interesting sound by attaching bright-colored ribbons or scarves that flutter when your baby kicks.

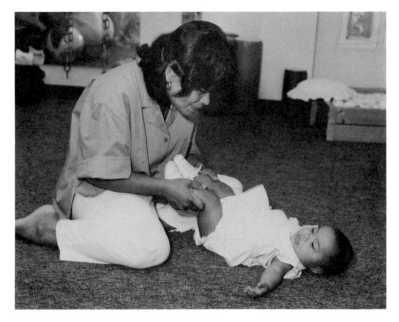

For babies who are physically impaired

Babies who are physically impaired are likely to be slower in attaining motor milestones and in gaining muscle strength, balance, and coordination. If your baby has cerebral palsy, spina bifida, or other neurologically-based impairment, early consultation with a physical therapist is important before beginning an exercise routine.

- Avoid sudden movements that startle your baby and make her jump, quiver, or stiffen up.

- If your baby stiffens her legs, do not bend them by force. Try to help your baby relax by talking to her, massaging her legs, or carrying her in an upright position. Once she is relaxed, help her flex her legs by applying steady and gentle pressure.

- If your baby enjoys a bicycling exercise but tends to cross or scissor her legs, place a small pillow between her legs before you begin that exercise.

- If your baby has tight ankles, flex her foot gently up and down several times a day.

- Avoid pulling your baby to a sitting position if she reflexively stiffens her legs and gets into a standing position.

- If your baby holds her hands in a tight-fisted position, play gently with each finger as a way to help her relax.

For babies who are hypersensitive or tactile defensive

- Find a warm room in the house where you can "dress down" your baby, place her on a sheet, and let her practice kicking.

For babies with Down syndrome

- Down syndrome babies tend to be flexible and flaccid. Massage your baby's arms and legs to increase muscle tone.

- Find different safe ways to carry your baby: place her in a baby carrier, cradle her in your arms, hold her upright on your shoulder. Each different position helps your baby strengthen different sets of muscles.

Reaching Out

At the same time your baby is showing an increased interest in manipulating objects, he is also learning to sit and crawl. This is a beautiful developmental synchronization that happens in the second stage, Reaching Out. Sitting up by himself frees both hands to manipulate toys, and crawling gives him the mobility to go after the toy he wants. As we give babies opportunities to practice these emerging motor skills, we increase their opportunities to play and experiment with objects.

Rolling Over

The ability to roll over from stomach to back and back to stomach may be achieved in either the Tuning In or Reaching Out stage.

- Roll your baby gently from side to side to get him used to the rolling motion. Sing a song to the tune of "Row Row Row Your Boat" to increase the fun.

Roll, roll, roll we go,
Roll from side to side.
Merrily, merrily, merrily, merrily,
What a way to ride!

- Help your baby learn to roll over by putting him on an incline. You can create an incline by setting the crib mattress on the floor and lifting it just a little on one side. Make sure to position your baby so that his arms don't interfere with turning over.

Improving Balance

- Use pillows or a swim ring to help your baby maintain his balance when he is first learning to sit.
- Use a large beach ball to further improve your baby's sense of balance. Hold your baby on the top of the ball and roll it gently from side to side.
- Bounce your baby on your knee while you listen to music or sing a song.
- Place your baby in a door swing. He will enjoy the motion and improve his balancing skills.

Leg Exercises

As your baby improves balance and coordination, he will be able to catch his own toes and use his feet for kicking.

- String a cradle gym over the foot of his crib so that he can kick it with his feet.
- Put different-colored socks on each of your baby's feet to increase the fun of foot-watching.

Crawling

Some babies begin to crawl during the Reaching Out stage. For a baby, moving about under his own power is an exciting step, bringing new horizons closer. To crawl, the baby must have enough strength and coordination to push forward with his feet from a prone position. A little encouragement will help your baby reach this important stage:

- With one hand, pull your baby's favorite toy just out of reach. Let your baby propel himself forward by pushing against your other hand.

- If your baby tries to crawl forward and ends up crawling backward, let him use your hands to push off.

- Place a blanket on a slight incline in the yard or park. Crawling downhill is easier than crawling on a flat surface.

- If your baby is becoming an accomplished crawler, increase the challenge by encouraging him to crawl up the incline.

Stage II Adaptations

For babies who are visually limited

Balance, like head control, is difficult for the visually limited child, who lacks the visual cues to help him with spatial relationships. (Try closing your eyes when you're standing on one foot and you'll understand the problem.)

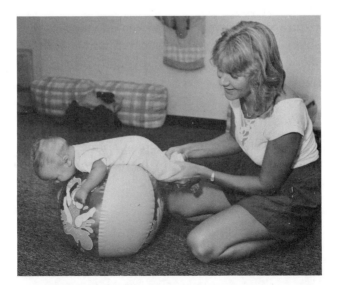

- After your baby has achieved some head control, he will be ready for a blanket ride or a roll on a large beach ball. Introduce these activities slowly so that he will feel secure.

- Begin balance exercises with your baby while he is safely on your knee to give him a sense of security. Once he is able to maintain his own balance sitting supported on your lap, give him a little push so he can learn to right himself.

For babies who are hearing impaired

- Continue to cue your baby by calling him by name before every exercise.

- Play music as you exercise your baby. Even if your baby has a profound loss, he will feel the vibrations.

- Help your baby associate changes in position with changes in your voice. Lift your baby up and down as you say this rhyme:

> *Up, up high* (use high voice)
> *Down, down low* (use low voice)
> *Up, up, up*
> *And down we go.*

For babies who are physically impaired

Swimming is a fine exercise for your baby as long as the water is warm. Introduce your baby to the water gradually. You may begin by pouring water on his hands and feet. Next help him splash with hands and feet. Then hold him against your body face to face as you walk waist deep in the water. Finally, turn your baby away from you and let him kick in the water. Continue to hold your baby firmly, and do not put his head under the water until your pediatrician approves. Talk and laugh with your baby as you play together in the water.

For babies with Down syndrome

Your baby may need help in developing sitting balance. A fun way to work on balance is to sit with your baby on a chair swing or glider, holding your baby firmly on your lap as you swing back and forth.

Making Discoveries

As babies make the transition from the stage of Reaching Out to the stage of Making Discoveries, their field of exploration is expanding. Once again there is a synchronization between the development of motor skills and social-emotional skills. Newly emerging creeping and walking skills allow the baby to explore more territory and investigate more objects. The emotional attachment to her care-givers keeps her within the safety range. A baby who has a good, strong emotional attachment to her parents is ready to explore new territory when her mother or father is constantly within view to serve as a base of security.

As you work to provide opportunities for your baby to practice her emerging motor skills, be sure to keep safety precautions in mind. With each new motor skill an infant achieves, there is a new set of hazards to guard against.

Creeping

Creeping is a more advanced skill than crawling. A baby crawls stomach-down like a turtle, pulling with her arms and pushing with her legs. A baby creeps on hands and knees with stomach off the floor. The best surface for a baby to creep on is a carpet. A textured carpet provides traction and keeps the baby's knees from slipping. If your baby seems to be ready to creep, dress her in soft and loose-fitting slacks or jeans.

If your baby is trying to creep but keeps collapsing, give her some practice with knee standing. Help her get into a kneeling position and hold her arms to help her keep her balance. Babies often learn by imitating each other. Invite a creeping baby for a visit.

Creeping, like crawling, has its own set of hazards. Stairs, doors to the outside, closets, and cupboards may be accidents waiting to happen. Babies who creep around the floor can also find small things and put them in their mouths, pull on lamp cords or tablecloths, and get their fingers into danger-ous spots. Baby-proofing the house is absolutely critical when your child has learned to move around the floor.

Pulling Up

Pulling up is a precursor of walking. When your baby is first learning to pull up, it may be an all-consuming activity, for parents as well as baby. Inevitably, babies learn to pull up before they learn to let themselves down again, and they can easily get themselves locked into a standing position.

The safest way for a baby to learn to pull up is by holding her parent's hands. For beginning pull-ups, support your baby's forearms or hold your baby around the waist. As your baby gains strength and control, she will use your hands to push off.

When your baby is learning to pull up to a standing position she may discover that a low coffee table is almost as useful as a parent's hands. Be sure to clear off the tops of low coffee tables.

Many babies pull up for the first time in their cribs. Often they find out that getting back down is not as easy as pulling up. If your baby gets stuck in a standing position, gently help her bend her knees to let herself down.

Bureaus and dressers are especially dangerous when babies reach the pulling-up stage. Your baby may open a drawer to pull up, and the whole dresser will fall on her head. Be on the watch at all times.

Beginning Walking

As a baby practices creeping, cruising (walking while holding on to furniture), and walking skills, she is learning more about her own body, what she can make it do, how high she can reach, where she can fit, and what she can climb. If your baby is slow to progress from cruising to walking, try the following ideas:

- Take your baby on a walk holding hands.

- Let your baby learn to walk by pushing a small, sturdy chair or a large box around the room.

- Increase her confidence by letting her hold on to one end of a scarf while you hold the other. After a while, just holding the scarf without you on the other end will be enough to help her walk alone.

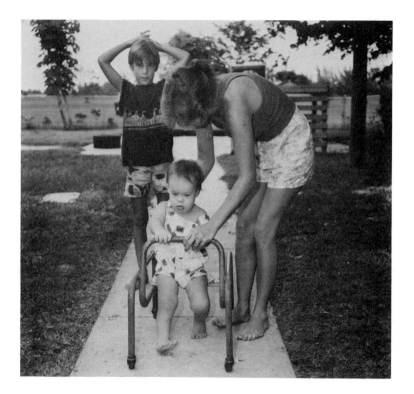

Once your baby is walking, she will be ready to develop a new set of more complex skills, like pulling a wagon, pushing a baby stroller, or walking with an armful of stuffed animals. Your child may soon learn to climb—a favorite toddler activity that requires very close supervision.

Climbing

Some babies seem to be especially good at climbing and will learn to climb before they learn to walk. Other babies will not begin to climb until they have mastered walking. All babies learn to climb up much more easily than they learn to climb down.

If you have stairs in your house, teaching your baby how to climb down the stairs safely is important. Even though you are careful about keeping the safety gate locked at the top of the stairs, there is always the chance of a slip-up. Teach your child to come down stairs on her stomach feet first. Begin the lesson on the bottom three stairs.

- Provide your baby with safe places to practice climbing skills. Use pillows and bolsters to create an obstacle course.

- Cartons of all sizes provide wonderful opportunities for practicing climbing skills. If you leave an empty carton within reach, your toddler will struggle to get inside. Because toddlers can find their way into grocery boxes, it is important that empty boxes be clean inside and free of cash register slips, or anything you don't want your baby to put in her mouth.

Although the early attainment of motor milestones is not related to precocious intellectual development, the mastery of physical skills contributes to skill development in other domains. The mastery of a new motor skill increases confidence and self-awareness and provides new opportunities for exploration and discovery.

11

Learning Language

Although it may be a long time before your baby can speak in words, the development of language begins at birth. Your baby awakens and cries, and you take him to your breast or give him a bottle. At first your baby does not know that his crying brought you to him, but after a while he makes the association. When your baby is a little older he will send out different signals, and you will be able to interpret them. You will differentiate the cry of pain from the cry of hunger, and the fretting sounds of a sleepy baby from the discomfort sounds of a baby in distress. As you respond differently to different signals, your baby is receiving his first language lesson.

Learning language involves learning the sounds of language, the meaning base of language, the grammar or syntax of language, and the rules of carrying on a conversation. Given that a baby must develop all these skills in order to communicate, the fact that children do acquire speech in such a short period is nothing short of a miracle.

A child who has learned language can abstract meaning from the language he hears and can express meaning in spoken form. He can also carry on a turn-taking conversation, where he both influences and is influenced by the words of the other person.

As we trace the course of language learning in babies and toddlers, we recognize stage-related changes just as we did in social-emotional and motor

development. We have once again labeled these stages Tuning In, Reaching Out, and Making Discoveries.

Tuning In

In the first developmental stage, Tuning In, your baby is making the transition from an inward to an outward focus. He is learning to organize his own behavior and attend to the events around him. When he catches sight of his fingers he watches how they wiggle. When he hears the sound of a rattle he searches for it with his eyes. At the same time he is becoming aware of his own ability to produce sounds. He listens to the sounds he makes and reproduces them. He engages in sound-making games with his parents, cooing, listening, and then repeating his coo. He practices a variety of vocalizations including grunts, gurgles, squeaks, and sucking sounds.

Increase your baby's attentiveness to sounds by giving him new listening experiences. Offer him different sounds such as rattles, squeak toys, bells, the tick of a clock, or the sound of a music box. Introduce some of the sounds in a quiet manner. Your baby may be even more attentive to quiet sounds.

See how your baby responds to sounds. When he is lying down, talk to him very slowly, then faster, and then slowly once more. Is he kicking his legs and moving his arms in rhythm with your voice?

Help your baby produce noises by himself. Hold a rattle in his hand and shake it up and down gently. After a while he will make the connection between the sounds he is hearing and the feel of the rattle in his hands. Or you can try making a rattle wrist band by sewing a piece of Velcro to his sleeve and a second piece onto a rattle. As he waves his arm he will hear the rattle jingle. The faster he moves his arm, the louder the jingling will sound.

Try some spoken sounds as well. Snuggle your baby comfortably in a position where he has a clear view of your mouth. Make pleasant vocal sounds with different mouth positions. Try "oo, ah, ee." Or extend your tongue and wiggle it. With a little encouragement, your baby will try to copy your mouth positions. You may even be surprised by your baby's cooing as he tries to imitate your vowels.

Bring your lips three to four inches from his ear and make the same sounds in a quiet voice. This gives him time to hear you at close range after he has just seen your face. Be sure to give each ear a turn. Talking into your baby's ear is especially important for the child with frequent ear infections or upper respiratory infections.

Try more complex sounds by holding your baby as you sing lullabies. Talk to him in highly inflected phrases with a loving tone. Avoid shouting or arguing near your baby. He is much more likely to practice his language when the sounds he hears are pleasant.

Allow your baby some quiet time to practice his own vocabulary. When you approach his crib, try to repeat some of the sounds you heard him make. Or let him listen to his own baby talk by recording one of his "conversations" and playing it back. Engage him in a playful activity that creates out-loud laughing.

Stage I Adaptations

For babies who are visually limited

- Your baby is missing some early language experience when he cannot see your lips. Let your baby feel your lips as you carry on a babble conversation.

- Some visually impaired children spin around in a circle or rock rhythmically back and forth. This is a baby's way of stimulating himself. It is a good idea to distract your baby with an interesting activity before he gets into a habit that is difficult to break.

For babies who are hearing impaired

A hearing-impaired baby babbles just like a non-hearing-impaired baby until he is three or four months old. Respond to your baby's babble with lots of smiling and touching. If your baby learns to associate his own babbling with your enthusiastic response, his babbling is more likely to continue.

Reaching Out

In the second developmental stage, Reaching Out, your baby is actually seeking out stimulation, initiating games, and actively making contact with the world outside herself. The back-and-forth conversations become more vigorous, and your baby is often the initiator.

As she continues with these back-and-forth conversations, your baby is becoming more adept at making different sounds. Soon her repertoire will include babbling and calling out, playful coughs, spitting and raspberries, and a variety of throaty sounds. Her babbling or repetition of consonant sounds will sound more and more like real speech as she experiments with changes in inflection. At different times she will seem to be asking a question, making a statement, or giving a command. Some babies learn to "sing along" with a familiar tune or imitate the consonant sounds they already know. Help your child expand her vocabulary by joining in her conversations:

When your child plays at making sounds, echo the sounds she makes. The exchange will encourage her to make more sounds and listen to herself. When your baby makes a playful cough, imitate her. She will enjoy playing a back-and-forth coughing game. Before she tires of the cough, change to a raspberry. See if she will change with you.

Make a new tape of your child's vocal play. Playing the tape will encourage her to talk back to herself and increase her babble repertoire. When your baby is babbling, position her in front of a mirror where she can watch her mouth.

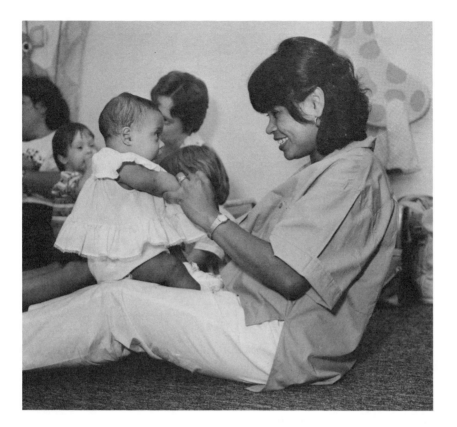

Your baby is learning new ways to produce language. She is also tuning in more to the language she hears. During this stage she may learn to recognize her name, react to "no," respond differently to different tones of voice, or listen intently when you are talking on the telephone.

Call your baby by name during feeding, bathing, and diapering. Substitute her name in songs and nursery rhymes.

See-saw, Margery Daw,
Georgia shall have a new master.

Play speech and gesture games with your baby, such as Patty-Cake, This Little Piggy, and So Big. Help her imitate the gestures by moving her hands until she learns the pattern.

Call your baby's name before you enter the room. Is she searching for you with her eyes as you enter the room? Start softly and gradually increase your volume until she responds. Be sure to repeat her name after she has found you with her eyes.

Listen to the consonant sounds your baby makes when she is alone in the crib. Make up rhythm songs to sing with her that repeat her newest sounds.

Pa-pa, Pa-pa, Pa-pa Jim,
Pat my nose and pat my chin.

Ba-ba-ba, ba-ba-ba, ba-bumble bee,
I ba to you and you ba-ba to me.

Da-da-da-da, da-da-da, Daddy Doo,
Da-da loves baby and I love her too.

Place a shatterproof mirror over your baby's crib or changing table so that she can watch her mouth as she babbles.

Stage II Adaptations

For babies who are visually limited

Begin to build your baby's vocabulary by introducing words that your baby can experience. Say "up" every time you lift your baby out of the crib.

Say "nose" as your baby feels your nose and "mouth" as she touches your mouth. Say "cold" as your baby touches an ice cube.

For babies who are hearing impaired

- Establish eye contact with your baby before you begin a conversation. Make sure she is watching your lips.

- Continue to show how pleased and excited you are with your baby's efforts to babble.

- As you sing to your baby, let her feel your lips and your throat muscles.

- When your baby makes a vowel or consonant sound, play back the sound into her ear.

- Keep a hand mirror in a convenient place. Let your baby watch her own lips when she plays with sounds.

Making Discoveries

In the third developmental stage, Making Discoveries, your child is making the transition from focusing on the sound of language to focusing on its meanings. Through vocal play, conversations, and back-and-forth language games, your child has become familiar with the sounds of language and with the rules of conversations—my turn, your turn, my turn. Now your child is ready to focus on the meanings of words and phrases and on the functions of language. In the months ahead, he will learn that language can serve a variety of purposes. He will learn to use language to ask questions, make requests, play games, give directions, and tell jokes. It will be many years before he uses language as the basis of thought and as a means of guiding his behavior or actions.

An important jumping-off point for learning the meanings of language is making the association between a word and the person or thing it refers to.

By now, your child may be attentive when you call his name. He may not realize that the name you are calling belongs to him especially, but he has picked up the concept that name-calling means "Pay attention." The next important step is recognizing that a particular name stands for a particular person.

Much remains unknown about the way children learn language. But there is general agreement that word meaning begins when a parent imposes meaning on the baby's spontaneous babble. The baby may playfully shriek out, "Da, da, da, da." The father hears his baby call and says, "Your daddy is coming." As baby happily repeats "Da, da," Daddy comes into the room. After a while the baby makes a clear association between his "da, da" babble and his daddy. This type of interaction helps the baby turn his babble into a meaningful word.

The expansion of language skills in the Discovery stage is associated with the baby's increased ability to imitate and recall sound combinations. When the baby is playing with a ball, Mother is able to say "Ball," and the baby says "ball" back. This allows Mother to help her baby make the association between the ball he is playing with and the word he is saying.

While your baby is improving his skills with word repetition, he is also getting better at expressive jargon. He is able to imitate intonation, the rise and fall of pitch and loudness, and can put a string of sounds together that sounds like a real sentence. After a while your baby will use these pseudo-sentences as a way of giving commands, scolding, or inviting you over to play. You can encourage your baby's emerging control of language by playing word games with him:

Play "body parts" and "show me" games with your baby. When you first introduce a "show me" game, choose something that is especially interesting to him, like a new pair of shoes or the "booboo" on his finger. Don't be upset if your baby says words wrong or makes up his own words for things. What is important now is the association of words with objects and people. He will learn the exact word later.

Exchange greetings with your baby. Say "Hi" when you come into the room and "Bye-bye" when you leave. Your baby will learn that words can stand for actions as well as objects.

Let your baby play with an unplugged telephone. The telephone helps your child learn the turn-taking quality of a conversation.

It won't be difficult for you to show your delight when your baby says his first words. Repeat these words after him and show him you know what he means.

Spend time every day reading books with your baby. Show your baby a picture album and point out pictures of the family. Make a scrapbook with pictures of familiar things.

When your baby begins to use single words, guess from the situation what he is telling you and expand his one-word sentence. If baby says "car" you might say, "Yes, that's a car." If your baby says "cookie" you can say, "You want a cookie?"

Say nursery rhymes with your baby. Even though he may not know what the words mean, he will enjoy the cadence.

Put familiar objects such as a ball, a shoe, a toy dog, and a rubber duck into a basket. Play a naming game with your baby. Ask your baby to find the shoe. Or name each object as your baby pulls it out of the basket.

When you are bathing, feeding, or changing your baby's diaper, tell him in words what you are doing: "I am drying your toes."

Even if your baby does not respond, continue to talk to him. Children who are slow talkers are most in need of language experience.

Stage III Adaptations

For babies who are visually limited

- If possible, buy a pet for your visually impaired child. A visually impaired child who enjoys the experience of petting a dog is likely to learn the word "dog" without any problems.
- Make a "feel book" for your baby. Say "smooth" as he touches the silk, "rough" as he touches the sandpaper, and "hard" as he touches the board.
- Name the food your baby is eating. Let him feel and smell the food before he tastes it.

For babies who are hearing impaired

- Listen to the sounds your baby makes spontaneously and find words to associate with the sounds. For "da-da," show him a toy dog. Repeat "dog" into his ear as he makes the dog walk.

For "pu-pu," say "Putt-putt, the little engine goes putt-putt." Let him play with a toy train. Show him a picture of an engine. Let him feel your throat and touch your lips as you say "putt-putt" and push the engine across the table.

- Always speak clearly to your baby and let him watch your lips as you talk. Do not use exaggerated mouth movements or talk in a very loud voice.
- Use gestures as you talk to your baby. It is natural to communicate with your hands, your body language, and your facial expressions as well as with your voice.

Language is a unique skill that differentiates humans from all other species. The development of language depends both on maturation and a critical set of experiences. This set of experiences includes opportunities to hear and practice the sounds of language, opportunities to hear language spoken in a meaningful context, and opportunities to practice language with a responsive and appreciative teacher. Your baby will benefit more from your talking with him about the mundane chores you are doing—particularly those tasks the two of you do together—than from an expensive "educational toy." For every child, the first and best language teacher is a loving, caring parent.

CHAPTER

12

Problem Solving

Newborn infants, whether preterm or full-term, healthy or at risk, have a built-in need to take in and organize information. This need to learn is as powerful as the need to take in nourishment. No matter how much food they are given, babies who are not held and played with cannot thrive. On the other hand, babies who are brought up in a responsive and enriching environment can grow and flourish despite incredible odds.

In this chapter we look at the intellectual development of children during the infant and toddler years. We discuss the development of both motor and sensory skills that help babies investigate their world. As we describe each facet of development, we suggest games and activities that parents can initiate to enhance emerging skills. Our discussion is organized according to the three stages of infant development: Tuning In, Reaching Out, and Making Discoveries.

Tuning In

During the first phase of development, babies notice and respond to a variety of stimuli. Right from the start babies have the ability to tune in to

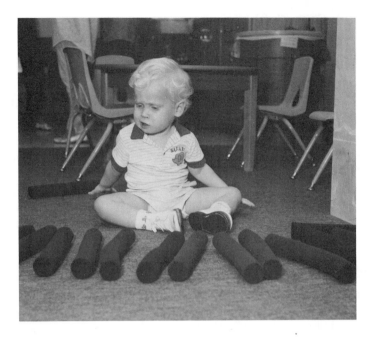

new information and to ignore information that is redundant. The newborn startles at the sound of a bell the first two or three times, then gets used to the sound and stops responding. When presented with a different sound, the baby will react again. This ability to discriminate between same and different, familiar and novel, serves as the basis for more complex learning.

Seeing, Hearing, and Feeling

Touch is the first and most powerful way you have of reaching your baby. As you touch and stroke your newborn, you are providing a special kind of nourishment that fuels infant development. Experts who have studied the effects of touch on the newborn recognize the critical role that touching plays in helping an infant organize her behavior and integrate her experiences. At the same time, touch serves as a control system. A crying infant can be calmed by a soothing touch, a drowsy infant alerted by gentle stroking.

Parents instinctively recognize the importance of touch and seek out opportunities to stroke their infant or hold her skin-to-skin. Some babies seem to crave this kind of touching, and parents describe them as being soft and snuggly. Other babies may show some resistance to touch and withdraw or show agitation when they feel the touch of a hand. When babies show distress at being touched, sensitive intervention is especially important. Slowly, gradually, and ever so gently parents must help their babies adapt to different kinds of touch.

Use gentle stroking or massaging as a way to help your baby quiet down. If your baby's skin is dry you may want to put baby oil on your hands. Make sure your hands are warm.

Rub your face against your baby's or stroke your face with your baby's hand. Her favorite feel is skin to skin. Fathers with beards should let their baby feel the inner surface of their arm. Short beards or "five o'clock shadows" may be too scratchy for a baby.

Your baby notices differences in tactile sensations and warms to a gentle touch. Tickle her lightly with a feather. Collect different fabrics in a box— silk, satin, suede, corduroy, wool—and let your baby feel the different textures.

As your baby coordinates the information from different senses, she becomes increasingly aware of where the parts of her body are and how they relate to each other. Let your baby watch as you tickle her arm with a dry, soft paintbrush.

There was an old belief that babies could not see until they were one or two months old. Now we realize that babies are not only able to see light at birth, but they can focus their eyes and follow a moving target. During the early months babies are developing their visual skills and are using their eyes as a major source of information.

Your baby's most exciting toy is your face. Hold your baby in your arms near the window so that the light is shining on your face, while your baby's face is shaded. Talk and sing to your baby.

Put a finger puppet on one of your fingers and let your baby watch as you move it up and down. Or let your baby focus on a colorful rattle. Move it from side to side while your baby is watching. After a while your baby will watch the rattle as it crosses from left to right and back again. When your baby has learned to follow the rattle from side to side, move it up and down, in and out, in a circular motion, and finally in a diagonal. Move your hand a little faster, watching your baby's eyes to make sure she is following the rattle.

Your baby will also enjoy watching objects that flutter and twirl. Hang a mobile over the crib. Make a mobile out of a colorful silk scarf and hang it in front of an open window, close enough for your baby to watch, but not close enough to touch.

Gauge your child's listening skills. Ring a dinner bell close to the baby's crib. Does your baby stop moving and notice the sound? If she has been crying, does she quiet? Squeak a toy near your baby's crib. At first she will appear to be listening, and then she will "habituate" or stop paying attention. When she appears to have stopped listening, change to a different squeak toy and see if she renews her interest.

Stage I Adaptations

For babies who are visually limited

Touching experiences are especially important for a visually impaired child. Take advantage of her quiet alert time to introduce touching experiences. Even if you think your baby cannot see, introduce visual games. Use bright colors with sharp contrasts or shiny materials such as aluminum foil.

For babies who are hearing impaired

Almost all hearing-impaired children have some residual hearing. Introduce the suggested sound games. If your baby responds to one or more of the games, redouble your efforts.

For babies who are physically impaired or hypersensitive

All sensory experiences, whether they involve feeling, seeing, hearing, or a combination, should be introduced gradually. The more tactile defensive a baby appears to be, the more important it is to introduce early touching experiences. Stroking your baby very gently while she is taking a bottle or falling asleep may be the first step in helping your baby enjoy being touched.

Remember that babies with a physical disability or babies who are hypersensitive are easily overwhelmed. Introduce new sensations one at a time. Proceed slowly and cautiously. If she startles, quivers, or tenses up, give your baby rest time before you begin again. If she appears to enjoy, or at least tolerate, your efforts at stimulation, continue for a short time and stop before she is tired.

For babies with Down syndrome

Down syndrome babies may not respond to sensory stimulation as quickly as other babies. Begin by introducing touch sensations. Use firm rather than gentle touching. Introduce a variety of feeling experiences: brush your baby's tummy with a paintbrush, use a spray bottle during bath time as a shower, and rub her arms, legs, and back with cornstarch or unscented baby oil.

As your baby learns about objects, the way they look, the way they feel, and the sounds they make, she begins to make connections. When you ring a bell over her head, she searches for it with her eyes. When you lean over the crib to talk to her, she responds with cooing and kicking. When you place a rattle in her hand, she may bring her hand to her mouth. As you watch your baby's reactions during the Tuning In stage, keep track of the different ways she responds to information received through different senses.

Reaching Out

In the Reaching Out stage the baby changes from passive observer to active participant. No longer content simply to watch and listen for the information that comes in, your baby becomes a busy and active investigator. Rather than waving his arms in response to an interesting sight, he coordinates his hands and eyes and reaches out to grasp the interesting thing he sees. As he grasps the objects around him, the baby is making a whole new set of associations—the rattle is to shake and the rubber ducky squeaks.

Object Play

During the Reaching Out stage your baby is making two generalizations on a nonverbal level. He is recognizing that objects can be classified or grouped according to functions—rattles shake, while paper crushes. He is also recognizing that certain actions can be tried out on different objects with different results. When you bang on the table, it makes noise. When you bang in the bathtub, there's a splash.

When your baby first reaches out toward an object he is likely to bat at it rather than grasp it. If the thing he is batting does something interesting, like spin around or make a noise, he will probably bat it again. After a while your baby will learn to use his hand to bring the object toward him. This reaching behavior becomes better coordinated, and your baby will adjust his hand in anticipation of the object he is reaching. After trying the object out "for taste" he will begin a more intensive investigation—turning the object upside down, passing it from hand to hand, and trying to make it squeak. Give your baby experience with a variety of objects:

- Watch your baby's reaction to a squeak toy. Some babies laugh at the sound and others show distress. If your baby seems to enjoy the sound, let him reach for it himself. Once he learns to make the toy squeak he will be ready to try a different kind, or perhaps he will try to bite the toy, making it squeak in his mouth.

- Give your baby the lid of a small plastic bowl. See if he will hold it with two hands or pass it from one hand to the other.

- Give your baby a washcloth to hold. When he discovers that shaking it doesn't make it squeak or rattle, he may try bunching it up and transferring it from hand to hand.

- Hand your baby several balls of different sizes. He will learn to adjust his hand as he reaches in anticipation of the size of the ball.

- Wrapping paper that crinkles holds a special fascination for babies. Watch carefully if your baby gets hold of a piece of paper. It could easily end up in his mouth.

- Put a patterned sheet on your baby's crib. He will make scratching motions as he tries to pick up the design.

- Curlers that fit into each other make an interesting toy. If you fit two curlers inside each other, your baby may learn to pull them apart.

- Improvise a cradle gym using large curtain rings, plastic brace-lets, and pot holders. See if your baby bats at the pot holders and grasps the rings.

As your baby reaches for and plays with different toys and objects, you will discover that there are certain favorite toys that he always comes back to or seeks out. This is an important development that signals the ability to recall specific experiences. If you watch carefully, you will see more and more evidence of your baby's increasing memory power.

- Half-cover up your baby's favorite toy with a diaper. Can he recognize it and retrieve it?

- Drop a colorful ball onto the floor while your baby is watching. Does your baby look down on the floor in anticipation of where the ball will land?

- Put a floating toy in the bathtub. Chasing and grasping it will be a challenge. Your baby gets better with practice—another indication of increased memory power.

- Using a piece of elastic, string a stuffed animal from the ceiling or curtain rods. As he tries to grasp it, your baby will laugh in anticipation of its springing back.

Stage II Adaptations

For babies who are visually limited

Give your baby extra opportunities to handle objects of different shapes, weights, and textures. Present objects in pairs that are almost alike. This pairing technique gives your baby early practice in identifying similarities and differences on the basis of feel. Here are some examples: a wooden block and a rubber block, a plastic ball with holes and a similar ball without holes, a squeak toy fish and a squeak toy duck.

Make your baby a texture box by turning a large carton on its side and gluing different textured material on the inside. Stringing bells from the topside can make it even more fun.

For babies who are hearing impaired

Play problem-solving games in a quiet room, preferably with a rug on the floor. Your baby should not be distracted when he is working hard to listen to your voice.

For babies who are physically impaired

If your baby has difficulty with grasping, find toys that can be grasped easily, such as dumbbell rattles, small cloth animals or dolls, and clutch bells.

For babies who are hypersensitive or tactile defensive

Use toys with bells rather than squeak toys. A high-pitched squeak can disturb a sensitive baby.

If your baby shows extreme tactile defensiveness and refuses to touch or pick up a toy, try putting baby socks halfway over your baby's hands. Your baby will shake his hands and watch the socks flutter. After a while he will adjust to the sensation of having his hands covered.

For babies with Down syndrome

If your baby is having trouble with a finger-thumb grasp, let your baby practice a grasping activity with a built-in reward. Make gelatin thicker than usual and cut it in cubes. Let your baby finger feed himself first with one hand and then with the other.

Making Discoveries

As your child reaches the third developmental stage, Making Discoveries, she is able to use her new skills and information to solve more challenging problems. She is interested now not only in the different ways she can manipulate an object, but she also is trying to find out how objects relate to each other. She is poking, prodding, pushing, pulling, and presenting herself with new challenges. She may puzzle over such questions as: I have a block in each hand already—how can I pick up a third block? Can I find my favorite toy on the bottom of the toy box? Can I pull open a cabinet door and play with the things I find? What can I find that I can empty or fill, pull apart, or break into bits? With each new discovery that the baby makes, you will find new areas in your house that need to be baby-proofed.

Help your child find new ways of investigating objects. Encourage her to combine her investigation in complex ways:

- Let your baby discover that some objects come apart and fit together. Improvise a stacking toy by covering two to three empty cans of different sizes with Contact paper.

- Let your baby watch as you bang two toys together, and then give her a turn. Let your baby extend her banging and pounding skills. Give her a short-handled wooden spoon and a kitchen pot. If she is really into banging, try out a xylophone.

- Let your baby discover the fun of filling and emptying. Give her tennis balls and a muffin dish, or let her put pom-poms into an egg carton.

- If your baby is ready for opening and closing, turning wheels, or pushing down levers, let her play with a busy box.

- If your baby has good control of her hands and is no longer putting everything in her mouth, you may want to let her scribble with a soap crayon, spread Crazy Foam on a placemat,

or manipulate peanut-butter clay. Pouring is a special skill that requires lots of practice. Begin pouring activities in the bathtub or swimming pool.

As your baby carries out her complex investigations of objects, she is learning through experience that objects continue to exist even when she can't see them or feel them. As she gains this new insight, she will enjoy playing hidden-object games.

- Hide a toy under a diaper and see if your baby will move the diaper to get the toy. Hide a toy behind a plastic tray. Will your baby try to reach through the tray, or will she figure out how to reach around it? Find a hard rubber toy that sinks in the bathtub. Will your baby reach into the water to retrieve the toy? (Bubbles in the bathtub increase the challenge of the fishing game.)

Here are some other advanced activities to challenge your baby's problem-solving ability:

- Give your baby a spindle toy. Placing a ring over the spindle is a challenge in itself. It will be awhile before your baby can put a spindle toy together with the rings in the right order.

- Puzzle play is an extension of filling and emptying. Home-made box puzzles are easy to make and even more successful than commercial puzzles. Start with a simple one-piece knob puzzle with a round inset or make your own puzzle by cutting out a square hole in a shoe box top for a block-dropping game.

- See if your baby can retrieve a toy by pulling on a string. Attach strings to her wheel toys. When she is in the highchair, tie a ribbon to a favorite toy. Will she toss it on the floor and pull it back up by pulling in the ribbon? Add a special element of fun by tying a bagel to the end of the ribbon.

- Put a doll or a teddy bear on a blanket close to her when she is seated on the floor. See if she will pull the blanket toward herself to retrieve the doll.

As your baby becomes more skillful with imitation and solving problems, she is laying the foundation for learning self-help skills. Children who have the ability to do things for themselves can cope with challenge without becoming overly dependent. We need to encourage such self-help skills at a very early age.

- Let your child drink from a cup. Several different cups are on the market that prevent extensive spilling and create a smooth transition from breast or bottle to cup.

Stage III Adaptations

For babies who are visually limited

- Give your baby extra practice with the concept of "inside." Get a set of cardboard stacking blocks. Glue different pieces of fabric on the inside of one or two of the blocks. Your baby will put her hand inside the block to discover the interesting feel.

- Make a shape game for your baby out of a large coffee can with a plastic top. Cut a two-inch circle in the lid and tape the lid securely on the can. Guide your baby's hand as she drops Ping-Pong balls through the hole. The sound of the ball bouncing in the tin adds interest to the game.

- Put a sock on one of your baby's hands. She will enjoy the challenge of pulling off the sock.

- Put something that your baby really likes, perhaps a toothbrush, inside a shoebox. Tape the top on, but make a large hole on one end of the box. Let your baby put her arm inside the "tunnel" to fish out the toothbrush.

For babies who are hearing impaired

- Play hide-and-seek with a transistor radio. Hide the radio behind a chair or under a cushion, turn up the volume, and see if your baby can find it. This will give her practice in locating the source of a sound.

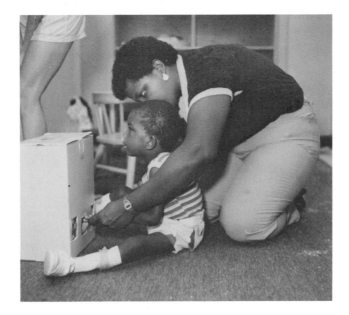

For babies who are physically impaired

- If your baby has difficulty picking up toys, place the toys within her reach in a flat box with sand in it. The sand will keep the toys from slipping away as she tries to grasp them.

- If your baby is not mobile, play a special version of hide-and-seek. Bury a toy in a box full of sand and see if she can find it.

As your baby becomes more active, you will find that he discovers his own problems and invents his own challenges. The more adventuresome he becomes, the more watchful you have to be. If he has learned to pull a toy by a string to make it follow him, he may try pulling the cord of a lamp, or the corner of a tablecloth. If he has learned about the fun of filling and emptying, he may dump out the contents of your purse and jewelry box or fill up the toilet with a stack of unopened mail.

After a while the explorations do become less vigorous, and babies begin to understand that there is some off-limits behavior. During the transition period it is important for parents to remember that their child is adventuresome rather than naughty, and that the experiences that babies accumulate are the basis for later learning.

PART IV

DECISION MAKING

Young parents raising children are constantly faced with decisions that affect the future of the family. Should one or both parents go to work? Where should the children go to school? How many children should we have? When there is a disabled child in the family, the decisions are likely to be much more difficult.

Section IV includes two chapters. Chapter 13, "Taking Charge," examines some of the issues and dilemmas associated with the selection of professionals. It also identifies some of the problems in communication between parents and professionals that can interfere with the parent-professional relationship. The chapter provides suggestions to help parents establish their role as partners of the professional.

In Chapter 14, "The Tough Decisions," we listen to parents of disabled babies struggle to make decisions when the issues are highly emotional and the consequences unclear. "Should we have another child?" "Should we send our baby to school?" "Should we go against the advice of our pediatrician?" "How can we plan for our baby's future?" Recognizing that every situation is very different and there are no clear-cut answers, we identify some of the factors parents need to consider as they go through the painful process of weighing the alternatives.

Whether you are struggling to stay "in charge" or grappling with a tough decision, parenting a disabled child is never easy. There are always pain and anxiety, but there are also special rewards. As you try to give your baby the best possible chance to achieve her potential, your baby helps you discover your own strength, resilience, and capacity for growth.

CHAPTER

13

Taking Charge

*"You know what I like about him? He always lets you know
exactly what's going on. He doesn't talk down to you, but he
doesn't use jargon either. When you ask him a question he'll take
time to give you an answer. If it's something he doesn't know,
he'll tell you so."*

When parents of disabled children talk about their interactions with
professionals, descriptions of good relationships are not as common as the
horror stories. In stressful situations communications are likely to break
down, and parents and professionals may blame each other for an outcome
that is probably nobody's fault. Unfortunately, the baby is the ultimate
loser.

This chapter explores ways of promoting the parent-professional partnership. The first section describes the physicians and therapists involved with
at-risk babies and provides suggestions for selecting a professional. The
second section focuses on the interaction between parents and professionals.
We look at both good and bad experiences that parents describe and show
how parents can work as partners with professionals for the benefit of their
child.

The Professionals

Parents of babies with developmental problems are often bombarded by specialists. Sorting out the functions of the different specialists and knowing what services they perform is important and not always easy. In general, specialists who work with disabled babies fall into four categories: medical specialists, nonmedical professionals, therapists, and social work professionals.

Medical Specialists

Pediatricians. Pediatricians are physicians who specialize in the care of children. Because the pediatrician is responsible for monitoring the growth and development of the child, he or she is the lead member of the treatment team. Pediatricians are certified as specialists by the American Academy of Pediatrics.

Neonatologists. The neonatologist is a pediatric specialist who works in a hospital setting with newborn babies. He or she evaluates babies who are at risk and supervises their treatment. Hospitals with intensive care units for high-risk infants are likely to have one or more neonatologists on their staff. Neonatology is recognized as a specialty by the American Medical Association.

Neurologists. Neurologists are specialists in disorders associated with the central nervous system. They are likely to be called in by the neonatologist or the pediatrician when an infant is suspected of having some type of nervous system dysfunction or seizure disorder such as cerebral palsy or epilepsy.

Orthopedic specialists. The orthopedic specialist is concerned with injuries or disorders associated with the muscular and skeletal systems. He or she may be called in to examine an infant suspected of having a birth defect or congenital disorder.

Ophthalmologists. The ophthalmologist is a medical doctor who specializes in diseases and disorders associated with the visual system. Pediatricians will ask for a consultation if there is concern about the baby's vision, or if there are medical problems for which an examination of the eye could provide diagnostic information.

Nonmedical Professionals

Optometrists. The optometrist is concerned with the diagnosis and treatment of visual problems. He or she measures visual competency and prescribes glasses when needed. The optometrist is not a medical doctor and does not treat eye disease.

Audiologists. The audiologist is concerned with the measurement of hearing. He or she uses a variety of procedures to determine whether an infant or child has any type of hearing loss or problem. When a hearing loss is detected, the audiologist may prescribe a hearing aid. Audiologists are certified by the American Speech-Language and Hearing Association (ASHA).

Geneticists. A geneticist is concerned with inherited or genetic disorders. The geneticist studies the chemical and physical nature of genes and chromosomes to determine how a disorder is inherited and the risks of its recurrence. Parents who are concerned about having a child with a genetic disorder can seek counseling at a genetic clinic.

Psychologists. A psychologist is a nonmedical therapist trained to observe and measure behavior and treat emotional or behavioral disorders.

Psychologists are responsible for assessing the baby's developmental progress and for helping the family with child management skills. The American Psychological Association is the professional association that certifies psychologists.

Therapists

Speech and language therapists. Speech and language therapists are concerned with the identification and treatment of speech and language problems involving the ability to reproduce language sounds, interpret spoken language, and use language to convey meaning. They are also concerned with potential speech problems that may manifest themselves originally as disorders in chewing and swallowing. Speech and language pathologists are licensed to practice by their state and are certified professionally by ASHA.

Physical therapists. The physical therapist is concerned with the child's strength, coordination, and motor development. In addition to physical therapy, the physical therapist can provide information about a child's muscle tone that has diagnostic value. Physical therapists can also help a family identify adaptive equipment, such as special highchairs, infant seats, and walking and standing boards that are appropriate for a particular child.

Occupational therapists. The occupational therapist is trained to work with a child in the activities of daily living. Occupational therapists help children attain self-help skills. They are licensed by the state and certified by the American Association of Occupational Therapists.

Social Service Professionals

Hospital social workers. The social worker is a trained professional with expertise in working with families. In pediatric hospitals or hospitals with neonatal or pediatric units, the social worker is usually a member of the treatment team. Part of the social worker's job is to take a family history, seeking information that might be helpful in understanding the baby's problem or in planning for follow-up services. Another part of the social worker's role is to help the family work out problems and identify resources.

Community social workers. Social workers who do not work in hospitals are usually associated with public or private agencies. In addition to providing family therapy, the social worker may lead a family support group or help a family develop a treatment plan. Social workers are licensed by the state and certified by the National Association of Social Workers.

Selecting a Professional

"I don't know how I lived through that morning. I had a C-section, and Marty came in my room. We didn't even get a chance to talk to each other when this doctor came in. I asked him how the baby was and he started beating around the bush—like he didn't have the guts to tell us. Thank God my husband was there. He looked him straight in the eye and told him, 'This is our baby, and we want to know the straight story.'"

One of the most difficult tasks for parents with a disabled child is to identify professionals with the expertise and personality characteristics to meet their special needs. The most common way to identify a professional is to ask your pediatrician to make a referral. This method assures a good flow of communication between the professional and the pediatrician, but there are disadvantages. If you are uncomfortable with the professional selected by your pediatrician, it may be harder to make a change. Fortunately, you have several viable alternatives.

- Ask your pediatrician to recommend more than one professional so that you can make a choice.
- Compile a list of the qualified professionals in your area who can provide the service you are seeking. Depending on the type of professional you are looking for, consult the County Medical Association, the Community Service Council, the state or county professional associations, the Yellow Pages, a local or regional hospital, a university or medical school, the school system, and/or the health and rehabilitative service departments in your area.
- If you belong to a parent support group, talk to different

parents about the professionals they are using. Ask specific questions about their availability to parents and their rapport with children. Ask the parents to describe how the professional benefited their children. Use the information from parents to adjust your list of professionals.

- When your list has been finalized, call to set up an interview with each professional. The interview can take place on the telephone or in the professional's office. Check the fee schedule and the insurance assignment policy with the receptionist before making the appointment.

- During your interview with the professional, provide as much information as you can about your child. If your child has an unusual problem or condition, make sure that the professional feels comfortable about treating your baby. As you talk with the professional, keep in touch with your own feelings. If you have confidence in the person and would like to work with him or her, you have probably made the right choice.

Developing Relationships with Professionals

"It was like yelling down a dark tunnel and no one was there."

Because having a handicapped baby is an emotionally charged situation, it is not surprising to find that parents are often angry with the physician who was involved in the original diagnosis. Sometimes the message is confused with the messenger, and parents project their anger on the bearer of bad tidings. Sometimes doctors who are charged with the responsibility of delivering an unwelcome message let their own discomfort affect the delivery of the message. Parents are occasionally too frightened to hear what the doctor has to tell them, and some doctors don't listen to parents' legitimate concerns.

As different parents talked to us about their experiences with professionals, we realized that some of the negative experiences could have been avoided if parents and professionals had given more credence to the parent-

professional partnership. Professionals would do well to abandon the "mightier than thou" attitude and recognize that parents have spent a very long time observing their own children. They know more about their own children than anyone else. Parents can benefit by taking a much more "in charge" position when they discuss treatment with the professional. The following list of suggestions may be useful to parents who want to take a more active role in planning for their baby:

- Set up an appointment to talk about the baby when your spouse can be with you and when the baby can be left at home.

- Make sure that the professional you are visiting receives the reports on your baby from other professionals before the visit. As an extra safeguard, bring copies of the reports with you.

- Write down the questions you have before you come to an appointment. It is easy to forget once you are there.

- Keep a diary of activities associated with your baby. Record telephone calls, prescriptions, tests, and office appointments.

- Be businesslike with the professional; ask about fees, credentials, and appointment policies. You are the consumer.

- If you want another opinion, or if you want to change professionals, don't make up excuses. Tell the truth: "We're concerned about Tina's progress, and we'd like to take her to the medical center."

- If you don't understand what the professional means, ask him or her to describe it again in different words. You have a right to know.

- Ask the professional for written material. It will help you review what you have been told and share information with relatives who were not at the appointment.

- At the end of an appointment with a professional, review what was said during the interview, including actions that must be taken: "I'm going to call you on Wednesday to report Gina's reaction to the medicine. You're going to call Dr. S. to make arrangements for the x-ray."

- If you feel that you did not get all the information you needed in an appointment, ask for a second appointment.

- Make a special effort to be on time for all appointments. If you have to cancel an appointment, do it as far in advance as you can.

In this chapter we have discussed the interactions between parents and professionals. Some of the suggestions that we have made may be difficult to follow because they violate the traditional dynamics of the patient-doctor relationship. The goal is not to undermine the relationship, but to strengthen it. As you assume the role of partner to the professional, you share your knowledge and expertise, and your baby comes out the winner.

CHAPTER

14

The Tough Decisions

In Part I of *In Time and With Love* we describe an interview study with 40 families with disabled babies. In this chapter we turn back to these families and look at the dilemmas they face and the decisions they struggle through. When parents meet in a support group, certain issues are raised time and time again. Should we have another child? Should we send our baby to school? Should we go to a different doctor? Should we plan now for the future?

Another Child?

"My husband and I are at loggerheads. Gina is two years old; she has cerebral palsy. My husband is convinced that we should have another child. He feels that it would be good for Gina to have a little sister or brother. It would get her playing more. I disagree. I can't imagine having another child. I am worn to a frazzle with Gina—carrying her around everywhere and running from appointment to appointment. There is no way I could manage another child."

"We have the same problem in our family, only it's the other way around. I want to have another baby, and my husband is dead set against it. I'm selfish. I'll admit it. I want another baby for me. I want to experience the joy of watching a baby smile when I sing a silly song or hearing a baby babbling away when I walk into the room. My husband keeps saying, 'How do you know the next baby won't be deaf?' "

"I'm pregnant now, and I'm not at all sure we did the right thing, even though we went through the amniocentesis and this baby is going to be okay. I worry about what it's going to do to Timothy. How is he going to feel when his little sister walks and talks before he does?"

"I can answer that. Andrew was only 16 months when Mercedes was born. Mercedes is the best thing that ever happened to this family. Andrew absolutely adores her, and my husband is like a new man. Sure, it's busy and the house looks like a disaster area half the time, but there's also laughter and silliness. And you know, now that we're not on top of him all the time, Andrew is doing much better."

"I could never do it. I could never have another child. I'd feel as if I were letting Terrence down. He needs all my time, all my energy, and all my love."

As we listen to parents struggling to make a decision, we recognize how complex an issue expanding the family can be. The fear, guilt, and self-doubt come to the surface again. "Am I capable of having a normal child?" "Will I still love this damaged baby if my new baby is healthy and well?" "Do I have the energy, strength, and desire to take care of another child?"

The decision about whether to have another child is a very personal one, and every family must grapple with it alone. Our best advice is to make no decisions until you have asked all the questions and talked out all the issues. Some of the questions can be resolved by talking with your spouse. Other questions may require input from your obstetrician, a pediatrician, or a genetic counselor.

Consider the question of genetics. Is your baby's condition related to a genetic disorder? If so, have you had genetic counseling? A geneticist can investigate your family and determine the risk factor for a particular disorder. If you do fall into an at-risk category, the geneticist will suggest prenatal testing. Fortunately, over three thousand genetic defects can now be detected in the prenatal stage.

What are the chances, according to a professional, of your having another child with a similar condition? If your unborn child has a similar condition, could it be detected *in utero* in time for a therapeutic abortion? Would you have difficulty deciding whether to have an abortion if you did find out that your unborn baby had a genetic disorder?

A second consideration is whether you are currently prepared to take care of a new baby. Given the expenses you have at the moment, how much strain would a new baby place on your budget? When you take into consideration the amount of time and energy your baby is taking now, do you have the financial resources and the emotional reserve to meet the demands of a newborn? If you delay having a baby now and wait until you are older, will you be capable of conceiving? How long did it take you to become pregnant before?

Consider the effect of a new child on your handicapped baby. Have you talked with families with handicapped older children and nonhandicapped babies? Were there serious problems of jealousy? Did the older child enjoy the opportunity to play with an active younger sibling? If you had a healthy baby to take care of, would it be easier for you to accept your first baby's problem?

Look at the big picture. Imagine your family with the new baby. Would your family have an easier time or a more difficult time if there were one or more nonhandicapped children in the family?

Sending Your Child to School

Parents agonize over the question of when and how to separate from the baby. They try to balance the needs of the baby and the needs of the rest of the family.

"You know, we can honestly say that since our baby was born we have never left her with anyone but my mother—and even then never for more than two hours. Sometimes I wonder if that is good for her."

"I have to go back to work—I can't afford to stay home, but I don't know how I could ever leave my baby."

"I was really resistant at first, but things are so much better since I've gone back to work. Alex is in a special program. He's there during the day and he's home nights and weekends. I come to him fresh and he comes to me fresh, and we enjoy each other more."

"I just can't do it—put him in a program at two years old. I wouldn't send a normal kid to school that young, so how could I do it to Jeff? He wouldn't have any way of understanding what was happening to him."

"I was really against sending him to school so young, but you know, it's been great. I can't get over how many new things he has learned. The therapists are so good, and they have all kinds of toys and equipment. I couldn't possibly do as much at home."

Placing a very young child in a program is a big step, and it is very difficult to know the right thing to do. Often parents are caught, feeling that their baby is too young to go to a school, but that if they don't send him, he may be closed out of a program. Before making a decision, ask yourself the following questions:

- Is there a high-quality program available in your area that would be appropriate for your baby?

- Does the pediatrician think that exposure to other children would affect your baby's health?

- If your baby were placed in a half-day or full-day program, what would you do while your baby was in the program? How beneficial would this activity be to you and the rest of your family?

- Do you enjoy being at home with your baby?

- Do you feel that your baby needs more stimulation or more therapy than you can provide at home?

- Are there other alternatives that you could explore in which your baby could receive the stimulation she needs without being separated from you?

- If you keep your baby at home until he is older, will you have missed the chance of getting him into a good program?

- Do you feel pressured by friends or relatives to make a decision that you are not comfortable with?

Treatment Options

Parents have to grapple with a confusing array of treatment options. Whether or not you have a pediatrician who is coordinating your baby's treatment, as parents, you are the final decision makers. Difficult decisions are up to you. Should you change professionals? Should you try a different therapy? Should you agree to give your baby a medication with the possibility of side effects? Parents struggling to make the right decision find themselves caught in dilemmas that are difficult to resolve.

"I read about this program that was developed in Philadelphia. My pediatrician is dead set against it, but I feel we have nothing to lose."

"The school wants our daughter on medication. They say that when she takes it she is much more subdued and easier to manage, but I just hate to give it to her. She's really out of it when she's on the medication."

"We've been tossed from pillar to post. Every time we go to a different specialist, we get a different opinion."

"The neurologist that we go to is absolutely set against physical therapy. He says that Tina is too young and it wouldn't do her any good. But I've seen other babies like Tina who have really been helped by a physical therapist, and even if the therapist did no more than show me how to carry Tina or what sorts of equipment to get for her, I feel it would be helpful."

The dilemmas that parents describe are very real. Part of the problem is that decisions are seldom clear-cut, and in many situations even the professionals do not have the answers. There are professionals who are misinformed or unethical who continue to make promises that cannot be substantiated. Often it is difficult to distinguish between false claims and genuine breakthroughs, and parents who will do anything in the world to help their baby are in a vulnerable position.

Making decisions that affect your baby requires careful deliberation. As you go through your deliberations, take into account the following points:

Before putting your child on a program or treatment regime that your pediatrician questions, investigate the program carefully. "It can't do any harm and it may do some good" is not a strong enough rationale. Any program that takes time and money and promises benefits it cannot deliver is doing some degree of harm.

Make sure that the people who are offering the program and treatment have the appropriate licenses. Call the local or state branch of the professional association that regulates the specialty area of the treatment. If it is a medical specialty, for instance, call the American Medical Association. Ask for the references for published research on the program or treatment. Testimonials that are a part of the program's publicity are not useful.

Talk with other parents whose children are currently in the program. Talk with those who have left.

If there is a special-interest group associated with your baby's condition, speak with a knowledgeable person within the association and ask about the program. Request literature or references. There is a listing of national associations in the Appendix.

Ask for an interview before beginning treatment and before putting money down. Make sure to find out the cost of the treatment and the expected duration. Call your insurance company and find out if the treatment being offered is covered by insurance.

There are situations in which a particular treatment or therapy meets all professional standards but may not be appropriate for your child. If you do not feel comfortable following your pediatrician's advice regarding a treatment or therapy issue, you may want to request a consultation for a second opinion.

It is extremely important to be up front with your baby's doctor before you arrange for a consultation. "My wife and I have given this a lot of thought. Before we go ahead with the treatment you have recommended we would like to have her seen by Dr. Z." In most situations you will find that your primary physician appreciates your honesty and will arrange for or support the referral.

Changing professionals is always difficult, and many parents find they want to make the change without letting the original professional know.

This is bad policy for several reasons. First, reputable professionals are unlikely to agree to see a child unless an appropriate referral has been made. Second, it is always important to have all the records sent on ahead before you see a new professional. You don't want your baby to have unnecessary tests or be given a treatment that has already proven unsatisfactory. Third, you don't want to burn your bridges. You may want to go back to the original professional.

When you decide that you would like to change professionals, be honest about the reason. "I would like to take my baby to ———. They have special expertise with autism." "I appreciate all you've done for the baby. For financial reasons, I would like to change to ———."

Questions About Medication

Decisions related to medication are generally made by the physician. It is up to parents, however, to ask in advance about side effects and to watch for and report unexpected reactions as soon as they occur. If you are uncomfortable about giving your child a medication that your pediatrician has prescribed, you may want to consider an outside consultation.

In some situations, the pediatrician will prescribe a medication on a trial basis. This is particularly true with medications prescribed to control hyperactivity. If your doctor has prescribed medication on a trial basis, begin by administering the medication at home where you can keep a record of behavioral changes and side effects. If your baby is fine at home without medication but is overactive or out of control when you send him to school, it is a good idea to go to the school and observe his behavior. Sometimes a child's behavior is quite different when there are other children around. It may be better to modify or change your child's program rather than to place him in a program where he requires medication.

From time to time you may read about a medication or other treatment regimen that your own physician has not prescribed. Show the article to your pediatrician. He may say that he hasn't heard of it but will make inquiries. Or he may say that the treatment is effective for some disorders but could be harmful to your child. Or the treatment could be perfectly safe for your child, but ineffective. Unless the pediatrician is fully convinced that the treatment you read about cannot hurt your baby, it is not a good idea to go against his advice.

Planning Ahead

Perhaps the most difficult and sensitive area to talk about is planning for the future. For many parents, just talking about the future is like giving up on their child.

"I don't want to hear about special schools and trust funds and how to make out my will. I can't even think about what I should make for dinner. Besides, I refuse to be that glum about things. Sure, my baby has a problem, but that doesn't mean he has a life sentence. I'm not giving up on Jimmy."

"Planning ahead doesn't mean you're giving up. You don't buckle your seat belt because you're planning to have an accident, and you don't make out a will because you think you're going to die. What worries me is if something did happen to Fred and me, what would happen to Gina?"

Unfortunately, even when parents do have the courage to look ahead, there are no easy answers. The best advice that we can give parents is to be as informed as possible.

To plan for your child's schooling, familiarize yourself with the provisions of Public Law 99-457, which describes your rights as a parent of a handicapped child.

Visit all the programs and schools in your area that might be appropriate for your child. Whether or not your child will be "mainstreamed," it is important to know what is available.

Talk to an accountant about setting up a trust fund. Make sure that you join a health plan and/or have an insurance policy that will not cancel out your child on the basis of a disability or a medical problem.

Make out a will in which you assign custody of your child to the people you feel are most capable of taking care of her. Make sure to rewrite your will if there are important changes in your family or financial situation.

Fortunately, most difficult decisions do not have to be made quickly. There is almost always time to gather information, consult knowledgeable people, and weigh alternatives carefully. Although there is never a guarantee that you will make the perfect choice, you will not go wrong too many times if the decisions you make are carefully thought out and informed.

PART V

RESOURCES

A

References for Parents

GENERAL BOOKS ON INFANT AND BABY CARE

Boyd, Richard D., and Susan M. Blume, *Portage Parent Program: Parent Readings*. Portage, Wisconsin, 1977.

Brazelton, T. Berry, *Infants and Mothers: Differences in Development*. New York: Pantheon, 1978.

Caas-Beggs, Barbara, *Your Baby Needs Music*. New York: St. Martin's, 1978.

Caplan, Frank, gen. ed., *Parents' Yellow Pages*. New York: Anchor/Doubleday, 1978.

Ferber, Richard, *Solve Your Child's Sleep Problems*. New York: Simon & Schuster, 1985.

Glazer, Tom, *Music for Ones and Twos*. New York: Doubleday, 1983.

Green, Martin, *A Sigh of Relief*. New York: Bantam, 1977.

Hagstrom, Julie, and Joan Morrill, *Games Babies Play*. New York: A & W, 1979.

Honig, Alice, *Playtime Learning Games*. Syracuse: University of Syracuse Press, 1982.

Jones, Sandy, *Crying Baby, Sleepless Nights*. New York: Warner, 1983.

Leach, Penelope, *Your Baby and Child*. New York: Knopf, 1978.

Levy, J., *The Baby Exercise Book*. New York: Pantheon, 1975.

Maxim, George, *The Sourcebook*. Belmont, Mass: Wadsworth, 1980.

Parents Magazine's *Mother's Encyclopedia and Everyday Guide to Family Health*. New York: Parents Magazine Enterprises, 1981.

Roman, L., R. Boger, C. F. Ostyn, and M. Veit, *Parenting: The Tender Touch*, volume II. Michigan State University, 1985.

Schrank, Rita, *Toddlers Learn by Doing*. Atlanta: Humanics Limited, 1984.

Sears, William, *Creative Parenting*. New York: Everest House, 1982.

Segal, Marilyn, *Your Child at Play: Birth to One Year*. New York: Newmarket, 1983.

Segal, Marilyn, and Don Adcock, *Your Child at Play: One to Two Years*. New York: Newmarket, 1983.

Segal, Marilyn, and Don Adcock, *Your Child at Play: Two to Three Years*. New York: Newmarket, 1983.

Sparling, Joseph, and Isabelle Lewis, *Learning Games for the First Three Years*. New York: Walker & Co., 1979.

PARENT BOOKS ON SPECIAL NEEDS CHILDREN

Apgar, Virginia, and Joan Beck, *Is My Baby All Right?* New York: Pocket Books, 1974.

Berger, Gilda, *Speech and Language Disorders*. New York: Watts, 1981.

Bisshop, Maryke, and Theo Compernolle, *Your Child Can Do It Alone*. Englewood Cliffs, N.J.: Prentice-Hall, 1981.

Cunningham, Cliff, and Patricia Sloper, *Helping Your Exceptional Baby*. New York: Pantheon, 1978.

Danner, Sarah Coulter, and Edward M. Cerutti, *Special Pamphlets for Special Babies*. Childbirth Graphics Ltd., 1986.

    NB40 Nursing Your Baby with Down's Syndrome, 12 pp.

    NB41 Nursing Your Baby with a Cleft Palate or Cleft Lip, 16 pp.

    NB42 Nursing Your Premature Baby, 8 pp.

    NB43 Nursing Your Neurologically Impaired Baby, 8 pp.

Dickman, Irving, with Sol Gordon, *One Miracle at a Time*. New York: Simon & Schuster, 1986.

Featherstone, Helen, *A Difference in the Family: Life with a Disabled Child*. New York: Basic, 1980.

Hale, Gloria, ed., *A Source Book for the Disabled*. New York: Paddington, 1979.

Hanson, Marcie J., *Teaching Your Down's Syndrome Infant*. Baltimore: University Park Press, 1977.

McNamara, Joan, and Bernard McNamara, *The Special Child Handbook*. New York: Hawthorn, 1977.

Norrohin, Margaret, and John Rynders, *To Give an Edge*. Minneapolis: Caldwell, 1975.

Pieper, Betty, *Straight Talk—Parent to Parent*. Spina Bifida Association of America, 343 S. Dearborn, Suite 317, Chicago, IL 60604, 1983.

————, *When Something Is Wrong with Your Child*. Spina Bifida Association of America, 1983.

Powell, Thomas H., and Peggy Ahrenhald Ogle, *Brothers and Sisters—A Special Part of Exceptional Families*. Baltimore: Paul H. Brookes, 1986.

Practical Advice to Parents. National Special Education Information Center, P.O. Box 1492, Washington, DC 20013.

Rappaport, Lisa, *Recipes for Fun*. Washington, D.C.: Joseph P. Kennedy Jr. Foundation, 1987.

Spock, Benjamin, *Caring for Your Disabled Child*. New York: Macmillan, 1965.

Weiner, Florence, *Help for the Handicapped Child*. New York: McGraw-Hill, 1973.

BOOKS ON PRETERM BABIES

Goldberg, Susan, and Barbara DeVitto, *Born Too Soon*. San Francisco: W.H. Freeman, 1983.

Harrison, H., *The Premature Baby Book: A Parents' Guide to Coping and Caring in the First Years*. New York: St. Martin's, 1983.

Henig, Robin Marantz, with Anne B. Fletcher, *Your Premature Baby*. New York: Ballantine, 1983.

Nance, Sherri, *Premature Babies*. New York: Pridon, 1982.

BOOKS ON LANGUAGE DEVELOPMENT

Austin, J., *How to Do Things With Words*. Cambridge, Mass.: Harvard University Press, 1962.

Barad, D.S., *All the Games Kids Like*. Tucson, Ariz.: Communication Skill Builders, 1983.

Brookshire, B., Joan Lynch, and Donna Fox, *A Parent-Child Cleft-Palate Curriculum: Developing Speech & Language*. Legard, Oregon: c.c. Publications, 1980.

Bush, Catherine, *Language Remediation: Workshops for Parents and Teachers*. Tucson: Communication Skill Builders, 1981.

Eisenson, Jon, *Is Your Child's Speech Normal?* Reading, Mass.: Addison-Wesley, 1976.

Johnston, E., B. Weinrich, and A. R. Johnson, *A Sourcebook of Pragmatic Activities*. Tucson: Communication Skill Builders, 1984.

Naremore, Rita, and Robert Hopper, *Children's Speech*, second edition. New York: Harper & Row, 1978.

Oral-Facial Clinic, *Cleft Lip and Cleft Palate: Questions and Answers for Parents*. Public Relations Department, Children's Hospital Medical Center, 300 Longwood Ave. Boston, MA 92116, 1976.

Reidlich, C., and Melanie Herzfeld, *0 to 3 Years: An Early Language Curriculum*. Maline, Ill: Lingui Systems, 1983.

Sklar, Maurice, *How Children Learn to Speak*. Western Psychological Services, 12031 Wilshire Blvd., Los Angeles, CA 90025, 1978.

Snow, C., "Mother's Speech to Children Learning Language." *Child Development* 43:549–565, 1972.

NEWSLETTERS AND MAGAZINES FOR PARENTS AND GRANDPARENTS

Especially Grandparents
(a newsletter for grandparents)
Kings County ARC
2230 Eighth Ave.
Seattle, WA 98121

Special Parent, Special Child
P.O. Box 462
South Salem, NY 10590

The Exceptional Parent
605 Commonwealth Ave.
Boston, MA 02215

Spina Bifida Association of America
Insights, official newsletter of SBAA
343 S. Dearborn, Suite 317
Chicago, IL 60604

Support Lines
Published by Parents of Premature and High-Risk Infants
International, Inc.
c/o Self-Help Clearinghouse
33 West 42nd St., Room 1227
New York, NY 10036

HOTLINES AND INFORMATION CENTERS

National Special Education Information Center
P.O. Box 1492
Washington, DC 20013

Closer Look
(information center for special needs children)
Box 1492
Washington, DC 20013

Parental Stress Line. Twenty-four-hour crisis counseling for those feeling overwhelmed by the demands of parenting.
1-617-437-0110

National Down Syndrome Society Hotline. Facts on Down syndrome, parent support groups in your area, programs for kids with Down syndrome.
1-800-221-4602

National Association for Hearing and Speech Action. Lists of speech/language pathologists in your area. Publications on language and hearing development, stuttering, common speech and hearing problems.
1-800-638-8255

Gerber Information Hotline. Nutrition, child care, allergic reactions to food.
1-800-4-GERBER

Beechnut Nutrition Hotline. Sleep habits, dental care, prenatal nutrition for pregnant women.
1-800-523-6633

Consumer Product Safety Commission Hotline. Publications on toy and nursery equipment safety and poison prevention.
1-800-638-CPSC

APPENDIX

B

Books and Records for Children

BOOKS ABOUT CHILDREN WITH PROBLEMS
(Appropriate for readers aged 4-12)

Adams, Barbara, *Like it Is: Facts and Feelings About Handicaps from Kids Who Know*. New York: Walker, 1979.

Brightman, Alan, *Like Me*. Boston: Little, Brown, 1976.

Brown, Tricia, *Someone Special Just Like You*. New York: Holt, Rinehart & Winston, 1984.

Buscaglia, Leo. *Because I Am Human*. Thorofare, N.J.: Charles B. Slack, 1972.

Fassler, Joan, *The Boy with a Problem*. New York: Human Sciences Press, 1971.

Kamien, Janet, *What If You Couldn't . . . ? A Book About Special Needs*. Scribner's, 1979.

Meyer, Donald J., Patricia F. Vadasy, and Rebecca R. Fewell, *Living with a Brother or Sister with Special Needs: A Book for Siblings*. Seattle: University of Washington Press, 1985.

Rosenberg, Maxine, *My Friend Leslie*. New York: Lothrop, Lee & Shepard, 1983.

SPECIALTY BOOKS FOR CHILDREN

Autism

Gold, Phyllis, *Please Don't Say Hello: Living with Childhood Autism*. New York: Human Sciences Press, 1975.

Hearing Impairment

Levine, Edna. S., *Lisa and Her Soundless World*. New York: Human Sciences Press, 1974.

Litchfield, Ada, *A Button in Her Ear*. Chicago: Albert Whitman, 1976.

Peterson, Jeanne Whitehouse, *I Have a Sister—My Sister Is Deaf*. New York: Harper & Row, 1977.

Wolf, Bernard, *Anna's Silent World*. New York: Lippincott, 1977.

Mental Retardation

Fassler, Joan, *One Little Girl*. New York: Human Sciences Press, 1969.

Lasker, Joe. *He's My Brother*. Chicago: Albert Whitman, 1974.

Sobal, Harriet Langsan, *My Brother Steven Is Retarded*. New York: Macmillan, 1977.

Smith, Lucia B., *A Special Kind of Sister*. New York: Holt, Rinehart & Winston, 1979.

Physically Handicapped

Fassler, Joan, *Howie Helps Himself*. Chicago: Albert Whitman, 1975.

Robe, Berniece, *The Balancing Girl*. New York: Dutton, 1981.

Stein, S.B., *About Handicaps: An Open Family Book for Parents and Children Together*. New York: Walker, 1974.

Wolf, Bernard, *Don't Feel Sorry for Paul*. New York: Lippincott, 1974.

Visually Impaired

MacLachles, Patricia, *Through Grandpa's Eyes*. New York: Harper & Row, 1980.

Sargent, Susan, and Donna West, *My Favorite Place*. Nashville: Abingdon, 1983.

RECORDS (grouped by artist)

Pat Cafra
> *Lullabies and Laughter* (A & M Records of Canada)
> *Songs for Sleepyheads and Out of Beds* (A & M Records of Canada)

Patty Dow
> *Fit Kids* (Cyclops Record, Inc.)

Tom Glazer
> *Music for One's and Two's* (CMS Records, Inc.)
> *More Music for One's and Two's* (CMS Records, Inc.)
> *Children's Greatest Hits*, Volume I (CMS Records, Inc.)
> *Children's Greatest Hits*, Volume II (CMS Records, Inc.)
> *Let's Sing Fingerplays* (CMS Records, Inc.)
> *Activity and Game Songs*, Volume I (CMS Records, Inc.)

Greg and Steve
> *We All Live Together*, Volume I (Little House Music)

Ella Jenkins
> *You Sing a Song and I'll Sing a Song* (Folkways Records)

Bob McGrath and Katherine Smithrin
> *The Baby Record* (A & M Records of Canada)

Hap Palmer
> *Tickly Toddle: Songs for Very Young Children* (Educational Activities, Inc.)
> *Babysong* (Educational Activities, Inc.)
> *Seagulls* (Educational Activities, Inc.)

Playful Parenting
> *Diaper Gym* (Kimbo Educational)

Raffi
> *Singable Songs for the Very Young* (Shoreline Records)
> *More Singable Songs* (Shoreline Records)
> *Baby Beluga* (Shoreline Records)
> *Corner Grocer Store* (Shoreline Records)
> *One Light, One Sun* (Shoreline Records)
> *Rise and Shine* (Shoreline Records)

Diane Hartman Smith
> *Loving and Learning from Birth to Three* (Joy Records)

Georgiana Stewart
> *Babyface: Activities for Infants and Toddlers* (Kimbo Educational)

APPENDIX

C

Toys and Equipment

TOYS FOR BABIES WHO ARE TUNING IN

Mobiles
Mirror toys
Toys that attach to the side of the crib to encourage visual exploration
"Happy Apple"—large, attractive plastic red apple to encourage visual exploration and lifting of head
Rattles—small handle ("dumbbell" type rattle)
Velcro rattles—attach to baby's wrists and ankles
Squeeze toys—soft and pliable
Crib gym
Puppets
Brightly colored socks for hands and feet
Musical toys—soft musical animals, wind-up TV and radio
Beach ball—for relaxation and encouraging lifting of head

TOYS FOR BABIES WHO ARE REACHING OUT

Language

Baby telephone
Books—sturdy pages with large, simple pictures

Jack-in-the-box
Dolls and stuffed animals
Puppets

Solving Problems

Roly-poly toys—hard plastic and inflatable
Musical instruments—using hands to make sounds (toy piano, drums)
Busy boxes
Rattles and squeeze toys
Pull toys

Motor

Balls—clutch balls, soft cloth balls
Crib gym
Large beach ball
Punch balls and other hanging items—streamers, wind chimes, kites

TOYS FOR BABIES WHO ARE MAKING DISCOVERIES

Language/Imaginative Play

Books
Play hats, dress-up clothes
Dolls
Stuffed animals
Plastic animals
Plastic dishes and cookware
Toy telephone
Cars and trucks
Small playhouse with little people and furniture
Puppets and finger puppets

Motor

Rocking toys (vestibular stimulation and sitting balance)
Riding toys
Balls—all shapes and sizes
Pull toys
Push toys—chime sounding, corn popper
Punch balls

Solving Problems

Filling and dumping toys—with large pieces
Inset puzzles—begin with one piece with large knobs (circles, simple shapes)
Shape sorter
Pounding toys—encourage use of tools
Scarves and boxes—for "hiding" toy games
Water toys—things that sink, float, pour, and sprinkle
Musical instruments—using hand or tool (wooden hammer, spoon) to make sounds
Jack-in-the-box

SENSORY AWARENESS TOYS

Sensory awareness activities encourage language development (through descriptions of materials) and awareness of the baby's senses. Playing with ice, for example, lets the baby hear and experience "cold," "wet," and "slippery." Sensory awareness games also provide fun and exciting play activities for the baby and parents to experience together.

Materials

A small bathtub or inflatable pool is perfect for sensory awareness games.

Feathers and feather duster
Corn meal
Whipped cream
Jell-O
Bubbles
Water
Cooked spaghetti
Rice
Textured materials
Crinkly acetate paper
Ice cubes
Soapsuds
Yogurt
Pudding
Records and music

SPECIAL EQUIPMENT

Crib

Sheets with interesting patterns
Tape recording of dishwasher—to stimulate interuterine sounds similar
to special records—or sound-producing teddy bears
Mirror (unbreakable) next to changing table, in crib, or on floor
Bright bumpers
High-contrast patterns on hanging objects and toys in crib
Toys with soothing tapes inside (heartbeat, swooshing sound)

Equipment for use during therapy and play

Remember to check with your child's physical therapist before purchasing
or using this equipment.

Inflatable beach balls
Small "rolls" (or roll-up beach towel or small blankets)
"Crawligators"—to encourage crawling skills
Wedge—to encourage weight bearing
Floor sitter—chair with stabilizing support
Inflatable tube for sitting
Large beach ball for relaxation and strengthening muscles

Feeding

Orthodontic nipples and pacifiers
Plates with suction cups
Soft-bite spoons, angled spoons
Training cups
"Ansa" bottles
Clothing with Velcro closures, roomy sleeves, and zippers with large
rings

D

Diagnostic Procedures

The brain is the message center of the body. Like a complex computer, it sorts information that is sent to it from other parts of the body, and it sends messages that direct the body's activities. If doctors are concerned about how a baby is developing, they are likely to order special tests that map the structure of the brain and provide information on how the brain is functioning.

Electroencephalogram (EEG). An EEG is similar in concept to an electrocardiogram. It measures the electrical signals produced by the brain. An EEG is used most frequently to identify seizure activity. Although an EEG is a useful measure, it is important to remember that 10% of the children with normal brain functioning have abnormal EEGs, and 10% of children with brain-related problems have normal EEGs.

CAT (computerized axial tomography) scan. A CAT scan is a special x-ray that provides a picture of the brain (or other part of the body). It is a way of looking at the physical layout of the brain. In contrast to an ordinary x-ray, which produces a photographic negative, the CAT scanner passes multiple x-ray beams through the body at different angles to generate a three-dimensional image of the brain. The CAT scan is used to identify brain abnormalities such as tumors, bleeding, infection, hydrocephalus (excess fluid), or other congenital anomalies.

Multiple channel physiography. A specialized procedure used to identify infants at risk for apnea or interruptions in breathing, multiple channel physiography provides an evaluation of brain, heart, and lung functioning and coordination. Babies who are found to be at risk on the basis of multiple channel physiography are placed on a sleep monitor with or without medication.

Magnetic resonance imagery (MRI). MRI is a new type of scanning procedure that utilizes magnetic waves. It provides a clearer image of the brain than other procedures, but is available only in select medical centers.

Protein emission topography (PET). PET provides a measure of brain metabolism. It has diagnostic value in that it identifies parts of the brain affected by disease states.

Blood work. Blood is an easily obtained and reliable indicator of the health of the child. A blood workup for babies is likely to include measures of hemoglobin/hematocrit (to estimate the number of red blood cells), bilirubin level (to determine the presence of jaundice), glucose level (to identify alterations in metabolism), and mineral level (to identify mineral deficiencies or imbalances). Specialized metabolic tests can also be performed to measure inborn errors of metabolism or the presence of toxins that could create problems (PKU screening is done routinely on all newborns.)

Spinal tap. Spinal tap (lumbar puncture) is a way of detecting spinal cord infection.

APPENDIX
E

Developmental
Assessment

Developmental instruments are used to measure the intellectual and notor functions of infants and young children. The major purpose of a developmental assessment is to determine whether an infant is performing up to expectation in accordance with his or her chronological age. When a child has had a slow beginning, measuring development at one point in time may not provide useful information; it is important to know the baby's *rate* of development. To measure the rate, a baby's development must be assessed at several different points over a period of time.

The Bayley Scales of Infant Development. The Bayley scales are the best known and most frequently used of the infant development scales. They are designed to measure development in infants between 2 and 30 months. The scales are divided into three areas: mental, psychomotor, and behavioral development. The Mental Scale consists of 163 items and the Motor Scale consists of 81 items. The Bayley scales provide a Mental Development Index (MDI) and a Psychomotor Development Index (PDI) that can be converted into age equivalents. The Bayley scales must be administered by a trained examiner.

The Kaufman Assessment Battery for Children (K-ABC). The K-ABC is a relatively new instrument designed to measure intelligence and achievement in children from 2½ to 12½ years old. It is divided into four scales:

Sequential processing. The child's ability to solve problems that emphasize the order of stimuli. Examples include digit span and the repetition of a number sequence.

Simultaneous processing. The ability to solve problems that require a holistic approach. An example is identifying a figure from an incomplete drawing.

Mental processing composite. The combination of Sequential and Simultaneous scores.

Achievement. Knowledge of learned or school-related tasks.

Learning Accomplishment Profile for Infants (LAP-1). LAP-1 is a criterion-referenced (pass or fail) test for infants from birth to 33 months. It measures performance in six functional areas: gross motor coordination, fine motor coordination, social, self-help, cognitive, and language.

McCarthy Scales of Children's Abilities. These scales are designed to measure the intellectual and motor development of children between 2½ and 6 years old. They are divided into six scales: verbal, perceptual performance, quantitive, memory, motor, and general cognitive. It yields a General Cognitive Index, which has a mean of 100 and is roughly equivalent to I.Q. The McCarthy scales are particularly useful with handicapped children.

Peabody Picture Vocabulary Test. This is a test of verbal intelligence designed for children from 18 months to 18 years. The Peabody test consists of a series of picture plates with four items on each plate. The examiner labels one of the pictures and the child is asked to point to it. The Peabody test is especially useful for children who can hear and understand language but who would not do well on a test that required verbal answers.

Merrill Palmer Preschool Test. This is an intelligence test for children 18 months to six years that provides age equivalents. The test items are packed in small colored boxes that the child is allowed to open. Most of the items have a toylike quality, so that children are likely to enjoy the testing experience. The Merrill Palmer is useful for children who are resistant to tests that are less fun, but it does not provide an accurate measure of a child's intelligence.

Stanford Binet Intelligence Scale. The Stanford Binet scale is the best known measure of I.Q. The older version of the Stanford Binet provides a single measure of intelligence derived from a series of subtests. The subtests are sequenced according to chronological age from 2 to 14 years old. The new version of the Stanford Binet (Edition IV) has a very different format from the older edition. In addition to providing a composite score that reflects general intelligence, it provides subscale measures of different aspects of intelligence—including verbal reasoning, abstract/visual reasoning, quantitative reasoning, and short-term memory.

APPENDIX

F

Organizations

ALBINISM AND HYPOPIGMENTATION

National Organization for Albinism and Hypopigmentation
919 Walnut St., Room 400
Philadelphia, PA 19107
(215) 627-0600

AUTISM

National Society for Children and Adults with Autism
1234 Massachusetts Ave., N.W., Suite 1017
Washington, DC 20005
(202) 783-0125

National Autism Hotline
Autism Services Center
Douglass Education Bldg.
Tenth Ave. & Bruce
Huntington, WV 25701
(304) 525-8014

ASTHMA AND ALLERGIES

Asthma and Allergy Foundation
1302 18th Street, N.W., Suite 203
Washington, DC 20036
(202) 293-2950

National Foundation for Asthma, Inc.
P.O. Box 30069
Tucson, AZ 85751-0069
(602) 323-6046

BIRTH DEFECTS

Association of Birth Defect Children
3526 Emerywood Lane
Orlando, FL 32806
(305) 859-2821

March of Dimes Birth Defects Foundation
1275 Mamaroneck Ave.
White Plains, NY 10605
(914) 428-7100

BRAIN DISEASES

Children's Brain Diseases Foundation for Research
350 Parnassus, Suite 900
San Francisco, CA 94117
(415) 566-5402, 566-6259

BRAIN INJURED

Association for Neurologically Impaired/Brain Injured Children
217 Lark St.
Albany, NY 12210

BRITTLE BONES

American Brittle Bone Society
1256 Merrill Drive
West Chester, PA 19380

Osteogenesis Imperfecta Foundation, Inc.
P.O. Box 245
Eastport, NY 11941

CEREBRAL PALSY

United Cerebral Palsy Association
66 East 34th St.
New York, NY 10016
(212) 481-6300

CLEFT PALATE

National Cleft Palate Association
906 Hillside Lane
Flower Mound, TX 75028
(316) 543-6623

Prescription Parents, Inc.
P.O. Box 426
Quincy, MA 02269
(617) 479-2463

Organization for Parents of Cleft Children
10 Carlsbad St.
Kenner, LA 70065

CORNELIA DE LANGE SYNDROME

Cornelia de Lange Syndrome Foundation
60 Dyer Ave.
Collinsville, CT 06022
(203) 693-0159; (800) 223-8355

CYSTIC FIBROSIS

Cystic Fibrosis Foundation
6000 Executive Blvd., Suite 510
Rockville, MD 20852
(301) 881-9130; (800) 638-8815

DOWN SYNDROME

National Down Syndrome Society
141 Fifth Ave.
New York, NY 10010
(212) 460-9330; (800) 221-4602

Association for Children with Down Syndrome
2616 Martin Ave.
Bellmore, NY 11710
(516) 221-4700

DWARFISM

Parents of Dwarfed Children
11524 Colt Terrace
Silver Spring, MD 20902
(301) 649-3275

Little People of America, Inc.
P.O. Box 633
San Bruno, CA 94066
(415) 589-0695

Dystonia Medical Research Foundation
8383 Wilshire Blvd., Suite 800
Beverly Hills, CA 90211
(213) 852-1630

FRIEDREICH'S ATAXIA

Friedreich's Ataxia Group in America, Inc.
P.O. Box 11116
Oakland, CA 94611
(415) 655-9833

HEARING IMPAIRED

International Parents' Organization
Alexander Graham Bell Association for the Deaf
3417 Volta Place, N.W.
Washington, DC 20007
(202) 337-5200

Children's Hearing Foundation
220 South 16th St.
Philadelphia, PA 19102

International Association of Parents of the Deaf
814 Thayer Ave.
Silver Spring, MD 20910

HYDROCEPHALUS

Guardians of Hydrocephalus Research Foundation
2618 Avenue Z
Brooklyn, NY 11235
(718) 743-4473

Hydrocephalus Support Group
225 Dickinson Street, H-893
San Diego, CA 92103
(619) 695-3139, 726-0507

National Hydrocephalus Foundation
Route 1, River Road
Box 210A
Joliet, IL 60436

IMMUNE DEFICIENCY

Immune Deficiency Foundation
P.O. Box 586
Columbia, MD 21045
(301) 461-3127

INTRAVENTRICULAR HEMORRHAGE

Intraventricular Hemorrhage Parents
P.O. Box 56-111
Miami, FL 33156
(305) 232-0381

JUVENILE DIABETES

Juvenile Diabetes Foundation International
60 Madison Ave.
New York, NY 10010
(212) 998-7575; (800) 223-1138

LAURENCE-MOON-BIEDL SYNDROME

Laurence-Moon-Biedl Syndrome Network
122 Rolling Road
Lexington Park, MD 20653
(301) 863-5658

LEUKEMIA

Leukemia Society of America
733 Third Avenue, 14th Fl.
New York, NY 10017
(212) 573-8484

LOWE'S SYNDROME

Lowe's Syndrome Association
222 Lincoln Street
West Lafayette, IN 47906
(317) 743-3634

LEUKODYSTROPHY

United Leukodystrophy
44105 Yorkshire Drive
Wayne, MI 48187-2859

United Leukodystrophy Foundation, Inc.
2304 Highland Drive
Sycamore, IL 60178
(815) 895-3211

METABOLIC ILLNESSES

Metabolic Illness Foundation
210 South Fourth St.
Monroe, LA 71202
(318) 343-0416

Maple Syrup Urine Disease Support Group
24806 SR 119
Goshen, IN 46526
(219) 862-2922

MUCOPOLYSACCHARIDOSES

National Mucopolysaccharidoses Society
17 Kraemer St.
Hicksville, NY 11801
(516) 931-6338

MUSCULAR DYSTROPHY

Muscular Dystrophy Association
810 Seventh Ave.
New York, NY 10019
(212) 586-0808

NEUROFIBROMATOSIS

National Neurofibromatosis Foundation, Inc.
141 Fifth Ave., Suite 7-S
New York, NY 10010
(212) 460-8980

PRADER-WILLI SYNDROME

Prader-Willi Syndrome Association
5515 Malibu Drive
Edina, MN 55436
(612) 933-0113

RETARDATION

Association for Retarded Citizens of the U.S. (ARC)
2501 Avenue J
Arlington, TX 76011
(817) 640-0204; (800) 433-5255

RETT SYNDROME

International Rett Syndrome
8511 Rose Marie Drive
Fort Washington, MD 20744
(301) 248-7031

SICKLE CELL

National Association for Sickle Cell Disease
4221 Wilshire Blvd., Suite 360
Los Angeles, CA 90010-3503
(213) 936-7205; (800) 421-8453

SPINA BIFIDA

Spina Bifida Association of America
343 South Dearborn, Suite 317
Chicago, IL 60604
(312) 663-1562; (800) 621-3141

Spina Bifida Association of Canada
633 Wellington Crescent
Winnipeg, Manitoba
Canada R3M 0A8

TAY-SACHS

National Tay-Sachs and Allied Diseases Association
385 Elliot St.
Newton, MA 02164
(617) 964-5508

TOURETTE SYNDROME

Support Organization for Trisomy 18/13
c/o Kris and Hal Holladay
478 Terrace Lane
Tooele, UT 84074
(810) 882-6635

TUBEROUS SCLEROSIS

American Tuberous Sclerosis Association
339 Union St.
P.O. Box 44
Rockland, MA 02370
(617) 878-5528; (800) 446-1211

National Tuberous Sclerosis Association, Inc.
P.O. Box 612
Winfield, IL 60190
(312) 668-0787

TURNER'S SYNDROME

Turner's Syndrome Society
Administrative Studies #006
4700 Keele St., York University
Downsview, Ontario
Canada M3J 1P3
(416) 667-3773

VISUALLY IMPAIRED

International Association of Lions Clubs
300 22nd St.
Oak Brook, IL 60521

Association for Education of the Visually Handicapped
919 Walnut St., 7th Fl.
Philadelphia, PA 19107

Retinitis Pigmentosa Foundation Fighting Blindness
1401 Mt. Royal Ave., Fourth Fl.
Baltimore, MD 21217
(301) 225-9400; (800) 638-2300

Retinitis Pigmentosa Association International
23241 Ventura Blvd.
Woodland Hills, CA 91364
(800) 344-4877

National Association for Parents of the Visually Impaired
P.O. Box 180806
Austin, TX 78718
(512) 459-6651

National Federation of the Blind
1800 Johnson St.
Baltimore, MD 21230
(301) 659-9314

WILLIAMS SYNDROME

Williams Syndrome Association
P.O. Box 178373
San Diego, CA 92117-0910
(619) 275-6628

OTHER HELPFUL RESOURCES AND ORGANIZATIONS

Advocacy Center for Children's Education and Parent Training
P.O. Box 10565
Raleigh, NC 27605
(919) 762-3451

Association for Severely Handicapped
7010 Roosevelt Way, N.E.
Seattle, WA 98115

Children in Hospitals (CIH)
31 Wilshire Park
Needham, MA 02192

Children's Hospice International
1800 Diagonal Road 600
Alexandria, VA 22314
(703) 684-4464

Compassionate Friends, Inc.
Box 3696
Oak Brook, IL 60522-3696
(312) 323-5010

Congress of Organizations for the Physically Handicapped
16630 Beverly Ave.
Tinley Park, IL 60477-1904
(312) 532-3566

National Easter Seal Society
2032 West Ogden Ave.
Chicago, IL 60612
(312) 243-8400; (800) 221-6827

National Genetics Foundation Inc.
555 West 57th St.
New York, NY 10019
(212) 586-5800

National Health Information Clearinghouse
P.O. Box 1133
Washington, DC 20013
(800) 336-4797

National Organization for Rare Disorders
P.O. Box 8923
New Fairfield, CT 06812
(203) 746-6518

Parents of Twins with Disabilities
2129 Clinton Ave, #E
Alameda, CA 94501

Sick Kids Need Involved People (SKIP)
216 Newport Drive
Severna Park, MD 21146
(301) 647-0164

SIBLINGS

Siblings Information Network
Department of Educational Psychology
Box U-64
University of Connecticut
Storrs, CT 06268
(Publishes newsletter for and about siblings, featuring articles written about siblings)

Siblings Understanding Needs (SUN)
Department of Pediatrics
University of Texas, Medical Branch
Galveston, TX 77550
(Publishes newspaper written by siblings)

Siblings for Significant Change
823 United Nations Plaza, Room 808
New York, NY 10017
(Information for families; refers siblings to events and services)

INDEX

About the Author

Marilyn Segal, Ph.D., a developmental psychologist specializing in early childhood, is professor of human development and director of the Family Center at Nova University in Fort Lauderdale, Florida. She is the mother of five children, including one handicapped child, and the author of sixteen books, including *Making Friends, Just Pretending,* and the four-volume series *Your Child at Play.* She is also the creator of the nine-part television series "To Reach a Child."

Parenting and Child Care Books Available from Newmarket Press

Baby Massage
Parent-Child Bonding Through Touching
by Amelia D. Auckett; Introduction by Eva Reich, M.D.

A fully illustrated, practical, time-tested approach to the ancient art of baby massage. Topics include: bonding and body contact; baby massage as an alternative to drugs; healing the effects of birth trauma; baby massage as an expression of love; and more. "For anyone concerned with the care and nurturing of infants"—*Bookmarks*. Includes 34 photos and drawings, bibliography, index. (128 pages, $5^{1}/_{2} \times 8^{1}/_{4}$, $6.95 paperback)

Lynda Madaras' Growing Up Guide for Girls
by Lynda Madaras with Area Madaras

For pre-teens and teens; an all-new companion workbook/journal to the *What's Happening to My Body? Book for Girls* to help girls further explore their changing bodies and their relationships with parents and friends; complete with quizzes, exercises, and space to record personal experiences. Includes drawings, photographs, bibliography. (256 pages, $7^{1}/_{4} \times 9$, $16.95 hardcover, $9.95 paperback)

The "What's Happening to My Body?" Book for Boys
A Growing Up Guide for Parents and Sons
by Lynda Madaras, with Dane Saavedra; NEW EDITION

Written with candor, humor, and clarity, here is the much-needed information on the special problems boys face during puberty, and includes chapters on: changing size and shape; hair, perspiration, pimples, and voice changes; the reproductive organs; sexuality; and much more. "Down-to-earth, conversational treatment of a topic that remains taboo in many families"—*Washington Post*. Includes 34 drawings, charts, and diagrams, bibliography, index. (272 pages, $5^{1}/_{2} \times 8^{1}/_{4}$, $16.95 hardcover, $9.95, paperback)

The "What's Happening to My Body?" Book for Girls
A Growing Up Guide for Parents and Daughters
by Lynda Madaras, with Area Madaras; NEW EDITION

Selected as a "Best Book for Young Adults" by the American Library Association, this carefully researched book provides detailed explanations of what takes place in a girl's body as she grows up. Includes chapters on: changing size and shape; changes in the reproductive organs; menstruation; puberty in boys; and much more. Includes 44 drawings, charts and diagrams, bibliography, index. (288 pages, $5^{1}/_{2} \times 8^{1}/_{4}$, $16.95 hardcover, $9.95 paperback)

How Do We Tell the Children?
Helping Children Understand and Cope When Someone Dies
by Dan Schaefer and Christine Lyons; foreword by David Peretz, M.D.

This valuable, commonsense book provides the straightforward language to help parents explain death to children from three-year-olds to teenagers, while including insights from numerous psychologists, educators, and clergy. Special features include a 16-page crisis-intervention guide to deal with situations such as accidents, AIDS, terminal illness, and suicide. "Parents need this clear, extremely readable guide . . . highly recommended"—*Library Journal.* (160 pages, 5½ × 8¼, $16.95 hardcover, $8.95 paperback)

Your Child At Play: Birth to One Year
Discovering the Senses and Learning About the World
by Marilyn Segal, Ph.D.

Focuses on the subtle developmental changes that take place in each of the first twelve months of life and features over 400 activities that parent and child can enjoy together during day-to-day routines. "Insightful, warm, and practical ... expert knowledge that's a must for every parent" (T. Berry Brazelton, M.D., Boston Children's Hospital). Includes over 250 photos, bibliography. (288 pages, 7¼ × 9, $16.95 hardcover, $9.95 paperback)

Your Child at Play: One to Two Years
Exploring, Daily Living, Learning, and Making Friends
by Marilyn Segal, Ph.D., and Don Adcock, Ph.D.

Contains hundreds of suggestions for creative play and for coping with everyday life with a toddler, including situations such as going out in public, toilet training, and sibling rivalry. "An excellent guide to the hows, whys, and what-to-dos of play . . . the toy and activity suggestions are creative and interesting"—*Publishers Weekly.* Includes over 300 photos, bibliography, index. (224 pages, 7¼ × 9, $16.95 hardcover, $9.95 paperback)

Your Child at Play: Two to Three Years
Growing Up, Language, and the Imagination
by Marilyn Segal, Ph.D., and Don Adcock, Ph.D.

Provides vivid descriptions of how two-year-olds see themselves, learn language, learn to play imaginatively, get along with others and make friends, and explore what's around them, and uses specific situations to describe and advise on routine problems and concerns common to this age, especially that of self-definition. Includes over 175 photos, bibliography, index. (208 pages, 7¼ × 9, $16.95 hardcover, $9.95 paperback)

Your Child at Play: Three to Five Years
Conversation, Creativity, and Learning Letters, Words, and Numbers
by Marilyn Segal, Ph.D., and Don Adcock, Ph.D.

Hundreds of practical, innovative ideas for encouraging and enjoying the world of the preschooler, with separate sections devoted to conversational play, discovery play, creative play, playing with letters and numbers, and playing with friends. Includes 100 photos, bibliography, index. (224 pages, 7¼ × 9, $16.95 hardcover, $9.95 paperback)

"Your Child at Play" Starter Set
Three paperback volumes, covering birth through three years, in a colorful shrink-wrapped boxed set. The perfect gift for parents, teachers, and care-givers. ($29.85)

How to Shoot Your Kids on Home Video
Moviemaking for the Whole Family
by David Hajdu

The perfect book for the video-age family and classroom—from the former editor of *Video Review*. Offers parents and teachers a lively, "user-friendly" look at making wonderful home-movie videos, featuring 11 ready-to-shoot scripts. Includes photos, index. (208 pages, 7¼ × 9, $21.95 hardcover, $10.95 paperback)

Lynda Madaras Talks to Teens About AIDS
An Essential Guide for Parents, Teachers, and Young People
by Lynda Madaras

Written especially for parents, teachers, and young adults aged 14 through 19, this valuable book describes with honesty and sensitivity what AIDS is, why teens need to know about it, how it is transmitted, and how to stay informed about it. Includes drawings, bibliography, resource guide. (96 pages, 5½ × 8¼, $11.95 hardcover, $4.95 paperback)

In Time and With Love
Caring for the Special Needs Baby
by Marilyn Segal, Ph.D.

From a psychologist and mother of a handicapped daughter, sensitive, practical advice on play and care for children who are physically handicapped, developmentally delayed, or constitutionally difficult. Topics include: developing motor skills, learning language, and developing problem-solving abilities; interacting with siblings, family members and friends; handling tough decision-making; and much more. Includes 50 photos, six resource guides, bibliography, and index. (208 pages, 7¼ × 9, $21.95 hardcover, $12.95 paperback)

Ask for these titles at your local bookstore or order today

Use this coupon or write to: NEWMARKET PRESS,
18 East 48th Street, NY, NY 10017.

Please send me:

Auckett, BABY MASSAGE
___ $6.95 paperback (0-937858-07-2)

Madaras, LYNDA MADARAS'
GROWING UP GUIDE FOR GIRLS
___ $16.95 hardcover (0-937858-87-0)
___ $9.95 paperback (0-937858-74-9)

Madaras, "WHAT'S HAPPENING TO
MY BODY?" BOOK FOR BOYS
___ $16.95 hardcover (1-55704-002-8)
___ $9.95 paperback (0-937858-99-4)

Madaras, "WHAT'S HAPPENING TO
MY BODY?" BOOK FOR GIRLS
___ $16.95 hardcover (1-55704-001-X)
___ $9.95 paperback (0-937858-98-6)

Schaefer/Lyons, HOW DO WE TELL
THE CHILDREN?
___ $16.95 hardcover (0-937858-60-9)
___ $8.95 paperback (1-55704-015-X)

Segal, YOUR CHILD AT PLAY: BIRTH
TO ONE YEAR
___ $16.95 hardcover (0-937858-50-1)
___ $9.95 paperback (0-937858-51-X)

Segal/Adcock, YOUR CHILD AT
PLAY: ONE TO TWO YEARS
___ $16.95 hardcover (0-937858-52-8)
___ $9.95 paperback (0-937858-53-6)

Segal/Adcock, YOUR CHILD AT
PLAY: TWO TO THREE YEARS
___ $16.95 hardcover (0-937858-54-4)
___ $9.95 paperback (0-937858-55-2)

Segal/Adcock, YOUR CHILD AT
PLAY: THREE TO FIVE YEARS
___ $16.95 hardcover (0-937858-72-2)
___ $9.95 paperback (0-937858-73-0)

Segal/Adcock, "YOUR CHILD AT
PLAY" STARTER SET (Vols. 1, 2, & 3
in paperback gift box set)
___ $29.85 (0-937858-77-3)

Madaras, LYNDA MADARAS TALKS
TO TEENS ABOUT AIDS
___ $11.95 hardcover (1-55704-010-9)
___ $4.95 paperback (1-55704-009-5)

Hajdu, HOW TO SHOOT YOUR KIDS
ON HOME VIDEO
___ $21.95 hardcover (1-55704-014-1)
___ $10.95 paperback (1-55704-013-3)

Segal, IN TIME AND WITH LOVE
___ $21.95 hardcover (0-937858-95-1)
___ $12.95 paperback (0-937858-96-X)

For postage and handling add $1.50 for the first book, plus $.75 for each
additional book. Allow 4-6 weeks for delivery.

I enclose check or money order payable to NEWMARKET PRESS in the amount
of $_____.

NAME _____

ADDRESS _____

CITY/STATE/ZIP _____

For quotes on quantity purchases, or for a copy of our catalog, please write or
phone Newmarket Press, 18 East 48th Street, NY, NY 10017. 1-212-832-3575.